I0455866

Lucifer's Great Book

By Lucifer Jeremy Damuel White

Lucifer's Book of Magic
By Lucifer Jeremy Damuel White

2023 (43 A.C.) San Francisco, CA.

"I am an unwilling devil. I cry like some vagrant child. I want to go home."
__Anne Rice– The Vampire Lestat__

INTRODUCTION

I am just setting out here to make a good book. One that presents the things that I have learned over the years. My wisdom comes from going back and forth from sanity to insanity. I have polished what I have learned. Have done so as much as I can instead of resting on any particular part, any particular phase it was in. In other words I have evolved my wisdom. I have been interested in many different religions in my time, each sincerely so. Including many forms of Christianity, Devil Worship too, but also Wicca, Buddhism, and have enjoyed carefully going over The Koran. It was the last five or six years of my life that I gained my best knowledge, knowledge of the occult and certain other things that cannot even be classified. A lot of what I know was not known before me. I was put on a rugged path of homelessness and madness for that purpose. I was meant to learn, to experience, and to share certain things. It is my purpose. I am a Christian Satanist. People respond to that in different ways. It really does stand out as a religious title. It just means that I am made from the two. I can fully appreciate the wisdom of God and His Son. Very well, the world is collapsing without that wisdom. They ask where God went, well, we tossed him away and ridiculed Him greatly. I have grown to become a philanthropic person. In so many ways, if you are into LaVeyan Satanism (have become lost and brainwashed by it) then this book is not for you. Which is to be expected, as those who have made cults will not tolerate alternative sources of knowledge. Honestly "atheistic satanism" sounds no less like an oxy-moron than "christian satanism." I am not here to riddle you with Christian complexities however, in fact I am against that. So many Christians want to instill guilt and judge people, splitting hairs over any sin they can. It isn't Christian to do so. In fact the first thing I will go over is magic and the occult.

This book can be read in any order of pages. It is not like a novel where the pages have to be read from start to finish. So simply open it up and read where you want to until you have taken it all in.

What I Know On Magic..

Here is magic that works. That you can depend upon. Some of it is a joy to use. Much of it is not found elsewhere, as I have created it myself. The occult has been my interest since I was just seven years old. My friends were discussing it in school and the whole thing fascinated me. Before I knew it I was reading every book I could find on it. Fortunately the library had a section just for it. My best knowledge of it comes from recent times when I was wandering the Earth and all its places, mad with Schizophrenia, experiencing things no other has before. You'll find unique things here. Sometimes strange things. Sometimes things that are fun. Sometimes things that are very helpful. And possibly even life changing things in this book.

Just maybe you will open that doorway that so many Magicians have sought to open. That door to power, to great things, fame, wealth, with your wishes coming true. The best and worst of people have opened that door in their lives. It is a life changing thing. Sometimes things have been revealed to me (visions given me.) I have touched upon the other side many times. Long lasting times, at times. So I have to offer such possibilities here for you, too. The opportunity for a more significant life.

I like to think that during my worst times I went into hell itself to collect the runes, so to speak. As was meant to be. As what it would lead to was many books by me, more than fifty at this time. Books that often teach magic but many other things as well. Such as philosophy and religion. So for my purpose to be correctly fulfilled I offer them free and have kept them all in the public domain. It is now a blessed life I live. One full of money and all good things. I cannot spare time to cease for too long and five years from now I could have written a hundred books.

With nothing more needed to be said we can begin.

Prayer Sheets

I'll begin with my favorite thing: a thing I call prayer sheets. During a time when I was homeless it was something I would do with my time. At the time I would just pull trash paper out of the garbage and write prayers on them, put them into a plastic bottle, with my hair inside. Since then I have evolved the idea greatly.

The basic concept is to include these: the prayer on a specialized paper (which I will explain in a moment), a tithe, and to preserve it. When I make my sheets I glue and staple ribbons around the border. Sometimes I print out an image that relates to my prayer, or simply an image of power for me, sort of like a visual idol. A lot can be used on a piece of paper. You can use stencils, stickers, different color pens, markers, drawings of your own, and whatever else you want to. The sheets can be preserved in various ways. They can be laminated. They can be rolled into a scroll and put into a bottle. They can be put into a zip lock bag and folded into an envelope.

Then there is the tithe. That doesn't have to be money. Money is great though. I like to use "world coins." That is, currency from all over the world. I buy a lot of those online as needed. However I also include things like rose quartz and green marbles. Those could be called "gifts" to include in your prayer sheets. I use about a gallon size bottle when I do it that way.

Then what? Well just throw it away. Such as when the bottle is full. Or if it is just an envelope. Or so on, when it is done then throw it away. The spirits you have called upon have read it and the rest is done. The cool thing is it will go to the landfill for who knows how long. Just don't put it into the recycle bin. My friend once told me it was like I was making a time capsule. I think it's almost like using the garbage to litter!

Supreme Visualization And The Principality List

I have another magic here that I have created myself. Overall I call it "taste magic." It is the occult/ Satanic equivalent of The Communion. Our's is more suitable with candy, preferably of different flavors and colors. You can use whatever food you want to. Candy just makes it fun and more convenient. Then there is the visualization component to it. First let's distinguish the simple minded kind of visualization from the occult kind. The simple minded kind has you thinking of simple peaceful settings as it is often taught by therapists. Like a peaceful beach, something like that. The occult kind on the other hand must evoke powerful inner imagery. Powerful feelings go along with it. You see things within your mind that you do not understand, you just know that there is power behind it. Then you guide these things into the world you wish to create, without, and within. That is an occult way of visualizing.

To put it together with the taste thing: each taste has its own thoughts. Literally like "food for thought and thought for food." If you have a particular wish then that has its own taste. If you have someone involved in your wishes then they are given its own taste as well. It is that simple. Consider it the fuel for your visions. You will in fact receive more and more visions in a natural way the more you practice taste magic.

Then there is *The Principality List.*

Person 1: Red, Hand, Staff, Bird
Person 2: Brown, Bear, Bee, Cane
Person 3: Green, Rabbit, Seed, Stage
Person 4: White, Goat, Ring, Thief
Person 5: Red, Whip, Cat, Fairy
Person 6: Wind, Lord, Yellow, Mouse/Rodent
Person 7: Bomb/Blast/Wand, Fox, Black, Beast
Person 8: Toad, Yellow, Horse, Dust
Person 9: Assassin, Creature, Word, Lion/Tiger
Person 10: Blue, Elephant, Spirit, Stone
Person 11: Mask, Dragon, Purple, Dog/Wolf

You and the ones you love make up a kingdom. This kingdom is seen in these. These represent each person within it. It can be just one, it can use all eleven, or wherever in between, too. The one rule is that the oldest person is the first and the youngest person is the last. So if you are the oldest then you are person 1. If you are the youngest within it all then you'd be the last in the list.

And these are seen in all movies and shows, all books, and all video games. They are an assistance and guidance for you. They bring you to an occult understanding that you will need.

They go well with taste magic and in fact were built *for* taste magic. There is nothing so well balanced as this. In case you are wondering, I am person four in this list. I created this list while in seclusion at a jail during one period in my life. I was alone there, in the small "rubber room" as they call it sometimes. The only thing in my whole life was food at that time. I strived to learn how to turn that food into a magical power and so I came up with the Principality List. A voice in my head later told me to call it *The Principality List.* Interestingly I later discovered the term is used by catholics to list the power of God's creation.

So whatever food I had I related back to my loved ones. It is made to describe food in certain ways. The color of it, most obviously. But a "cane" can be any stick food. Can also mean "sugar cane." "Whip" can be cream. "Dust" can be instant drink powder. Of course "seed" can mean those seeds you eat. "Stone" can be hard candy, and so on.

My Most Favorite Vision

Early one morning while homeless I laid down on the grass of a park. It was the time of twilight for the sky above. The morning star (Venus) was still shining a bit. Then some strange thing started happening. A black looking cloud that looked like a bat angel appeared from below venus. It went to the east turning into what looked like a serpent. It went right over the first rays of the sun somewhere to the East. Then a white cloud appeared below Venus, one looking upward, and one more like a magnificent bird. After that a cloud that looked like a black rainbow appeared in the upper western part of the sky. Then a murder of crows flocked into the sky, scattering. The volume of them was pronounced. After which the Church bell tolled again and again.

A Pilgrimage For Greatness

Sometimes becoming a great magician requires that you step out on the ledge. To be willing to submit to it fully in faith. If we have a pampered and nurtured life then our spirit remains weak. Our power within remains weak. But to radically change your life takes power and courage. It was like Buddha himself. He had a great life. But he wanted more and would leave his home to inherit nothing (which is not at all true, becoming the person he did.)

I had been homeless basically for years going into about every type of home you can imagine: a group home, a boarding care, a friend's home, a friend's shack, father's shack, room mates, jail, mental hospital, field, bench, trailer, apartment, home, you name it. When I became downright homeless I decided to go to San Francisco. It was not even so hard on me. My schizophrenia taught me many things. Was a bittersweet thing in so many ways. It wasn't until I got back on medication that I could gather my thoughts and put them into my writings the right way. I had left quite a poor state anyways: New Mexico.

It is a "more you seek the more you find" kind of thing. Before all of this I didn't do things so drastically but they did assist me in gaining a connection to the metaphysical. Such as taking long walks into the desert of Arizona, meditating along the way. I was always trying to contact Satan. Then on my 18th birthday something remarkable happened: I did. During my birthday, my family and I went to a park outside of town. Off in the distance there was a group camping out. As it turns out they were mostly composed of Satanists. And it was there that I met Satan for the first time!

Idols

We make them all the time without even knowing that we do. They are not limited to golden cows. They are not even limited to officially recognized deities. No, I say that even a StarBucks sign is an idol, or a McDonnald's Arch. The place where they sacrifice and prepare your beef with a side of toys which themselves are idols. Yes, action figures make good idols! I like the ones that resemble typical devils in one way or another. Strangely enough only the troll dolls are called out on it, by Christians. I think there are figures more diabolical looking than those.

I have a story to illustrate the point: When I was 19 years old (in 1999) a Final Fantasy 9 commercial came on TV. Being as I was and given the time, I was astounded by it. You have to understand that often our first exposure to these things was during a commercial. We didn't have the internet to see it well ahead of time. Anyways, I felt so compelled to draw an image of Quistis. I didn't even know a lot about her but I worshiped her. I was in reality drawing an idol. Maybe popular singers and actors are called "idols" for a good reason. They present a kind of image. They carry along their own hymns in many ways. They act in ritual in many ways too, the process of acting itself.

If all I have is a StarBucks cup then I will use it towards magic. At one time those were like chalices to me.

Obscuria

Let your magic come from obscure sources and it will be entirely your own. Look into a forgotten past to do so. Operating in a unique way is a great magic power to have. In a sea of sameness be different: that is the embodiment of magic itself. You will then not work like others but will work as a sole being. You will find yourself in places that are long dusted over. Like in a film about the cave containing treasures, so you will find yourself. Who wants to hear what all others are saying anyway? Who wants to go the way that all others are led? It is the difference between being a crystal (at best, more often just a dumb stone) or being a diamond.

Magical Ununciation

Speaking in tongues for a magician is taught here: First, let's go over picking a new name. A good magician should have a good name. You can pick one already there but be warned that such names come at a stiff price. Let me elaborate with the cost of my own. For taking the name *Lucifer* I had my skull cracked. When someone would not call me Lucifer I spat in his face. This giant of a person. He struck me so hard that I flew backwards and landed on the ground, losing a pint of blood. I got right back up on my feet at least. The crack on my skull is right where my third eye would be. So believe me, taking a high name does not come free.

      The second means to find your name is by making new words basically. Just like sounds are put together to mean more than one thing, a name can be made in a similar way. If you want to make the name "person of light" then that could be "Personalit." Light doesn't have to be light. It can be the word Ray, or Shine, or something else. If you like Shiva and Satan and serve them, then the name could be "Shatan," if Lilith and Satan, then "Shalith."

      There is often the "The" among us. Such as "The Barbarian," "The Destroyer," or "The Thief." Such a title normally comes after the name we have taken. I have chosen the last name of White for a couple of reasons. It is a way of saying gray when you include it after the name of Lucifer. For me, black was just too easy. It is the color adored by so many Satanists. My other reason is that the best food and things are white (lighting, clouds, stars, the moon, the hottest temperature, the snow, sugar, salt, to say the least.) Though nothing beats being driven in a vehicle in the deep darkness overnight.

      These things go beyond names. We have often seen among magicians the use of a strange mix of non language words. That is a magical language. It is personally known by the magician. To others it may come across as nonsense but for them it all means something. As something carefully put together. It is a way of speaking to divinities. They can be formed into chants. They are powerful as such. They could be a word to focus on over a period. To repeat it over and over again while building up power. In any case they should be words that evoke feeling and power from its speaker. If others are to use the words themselves then they should be well prepared to use them correctly.

Bright Sided Thinking and Optimal-Pathic Reasoning

Bright sided thinking and optimal pathic reasoning are a source of magic power. Optimal pathic reasoning is a word that means reasoning in its brightest sense. It is to see even bad things as good: to look for answers at least. To see how something may not even be bad as one may think. To see the sun through the clouds, so to speak. It is to see the silver lining in the clouds. The principle is that what we reason comes to fruition and can either make us or break us, bless us or curse us.

For that sake incorporate into it these things: gratitude (counting your blessings), appreciate all that is well in your life, adore the things you own, look forward to future things, make a bad thing into a good thing where possible, have pride, as much pride as possible, and do these until you are drunk with good feelings, drunk with optimism, pride, and such things. Do some "pacing." Not "pacing" in the negative sense (which psychologists seem to think can only indicate a nervous person) but as a person building up "happy power." "Ego power," you could say.

At my own personal best I used to be able to do it all day. Going down the long hallways until a loud and thunderous storm would appear.

Being Resourceful

Some use poker cards as Tarot cards. I used to go to Buddhist/Hindu idol stores to pray to the idols there. When all I had for music came from a pocket radio I began making the music mean things it wasn't meant to mean. I wanted metal or something else, after all. I once saw this thing out in the city. It was a metallic pig face with a bowl underneath it. Looked just like an altar. When I was younger I substituted a bell for a keyboard. In a time with no internet things like that were actually hard to come by. Those and things like black candles. I made a black candle once with a goldfish fish bowl, several different colors of candles, and a shoestring. Then there were the prayer sheets I mentioned earlier. I'd take trash paper from the garbage and write out prayers on them. I wanted to practice magic at times but was very limited for one reason or another.

The True Definition of Hell

Hell isn't a place. It is a state that one is in. It is a type of presence around and within. So a person can be in hell while all those around them are not. And I am not talking about the way people say "it was hell." That wasn't hell, just hardship. Hell is a far more complex state than that. There are certain characteristics of it that I will go over. First, you are much more sensitive when in hell. Everything is more pronounced. What is not sensed in regular existence is heavily sensed in hell. If someone has a sultry voice, or seems a little strange, you will certainly hear it in their voice. As a result, music sounds strange. There is no getting over how strange the sounds sound and the singer's voice often sounds downright diabolical.

Second, fantasy is reality. There is truth to fantasy. In the existence of hell one can truly go down the rabbit's hole. These include visions. They include the fact that magic is much more potent there and more fully realized. Sorts of messages come at you, as in a theme.

Third, it can be agonizing. You might get lost in all of it. You might spend the entire night trying to perfectly draw the perfect image in obsession. It can also be highly pleasurable however. You could become enraptured by music. Your feelings are much stronger in general. Your senses are heightened as well. In a way that makes soda taste toxic. In a way that tuna straight from the can is devoured, and its liquid drunk. In a way that you wish to pour laundry detergent on your carpet.

These are some of the things that truly make up what Hell is like. It is not a condition that most will ever enter into, not in human form.

Lost Values

Continuing with different subjects, "lost values" is a good place to start.

What values have we lost in the modern world? I would list these:

Strength- It is more expected of people to be weak. It is in fact sometimes essential if you are to be treated fairly– and if you are to reap in the rewards that have been set up for such people.

Maturity- This is a big one. It has never been so important to be mature than it is these days. People can get themselves into all sorts of trouble, and have, again and again, in modern times. People like those who would vandalize and get into fights over one small matter or another.

Patience- Patience sums up so many important virtues. With patience we work, we clean, we don't boil over with anger. We get things done instead of "rage quitting." It can be a bit of an annoyance to wait your turn but trust me, you will feel much better if you see it through than if you just walk out over frustration.

Understanding- I had a hell of a time getting my medication the last time. They have a delivery service. They said they can't guarantee it will arrive on the day I called it in. The way it is there is a large window of when it may arrive. So I waited around hoping for it to get to my door. It didn't get there that day. It was the new year's Holliday after that and I could only wait. I called back a few days later and as soon as they said "we can't guarantee it will get there" I said I would pick it up myself. They said it will be ready when I get there. The bus ride was about an hour long. When I got there it wasn't ready. So I waited around awhile. Then they packaged my medication and apologized for the wait. I told them that I understand and that I know they've been busy lately.

Hard Work- In so many ways modern tools have enabled people to create things so easily. I think that it shows though. I am into old gaming stuff and when I saw a video about a new Nintendo 64 video game being made (a game made for a system that has long been out of production) I think I knew what to expect and was right. The graphics were a simplistic mess. They could barely be called 16-bit level graphics. I kind of find it insulting in fact.

Truthfulness- People will lie tooth and nail to get out of problems and rehearse their lies again and again until the right fit is found. It is a problem that goes back to the Garden. I watch interrogation videos sometimes, of terrible people. They squirm and they adjust what they are saying, trying to pull off gymnastics with their deceit. As for me if I am lied to once then I just cannot trust a person anymore.

Self Restraint- In a world of selfishness and singular superiority, of hedonism, of such things as have been largely taught by modern psychologists, it is to be expected. It is to be expected that people only serve their own needs as though the world only exists when they enter into the room. People are taught to not hold back their sexual urges calling it "harmful repression." The same goes with anger. If you hold it back then presumably it will blow over "like a volcano." But that is all such nonsense and only teaches people to be hateful and perverted.

The Most Important Lessons In Life And The Emergence of Satan's Children

New Satanic Age = Satanic Children. Modern adults are like children. Some of us have been maturing all along but the majority have not. Satanic things have taken over the airways. Things are being sorted out but at the moment it is like a new found life, a different existence than that of the past Christian Eras. We find ourselves in a sort of Earthly paradise. One of pleasure seeking and materialism. Life has come to mean more than anything spiritual could offer. We no longer live in shambles staring out at the nighttime stars, having to work most of the time. Instead we have a great big world all around us. With our freedom of speech we have created things clearly more Satanic, and more so all the time– often in the form of cartoons and video games. We have found a playground on Earth. A great place that no religion could sensibly take from us. The behavior of modern people shows it, too. We have come to a point where we must rethink almost everything. Old laws that were thought at one time to exist forever are quickly being undone. New rights emerge, thoughtfully, replacing them. We can't have things taken from us and if we do, we act like babies. The old moral code cannot stand. Things that were at one time forbidden are now encouraged, even celebrated.

New frontiers are found everywhere. So what about the future? The future is the result of ages of development. For untold sums of time that evolution was a thing of addition, now, it is a thing of multiplication. It is like our God: progress. To progress we depend. Progress will save everything. It will save us. It will deter crime, feed one and everybody, do our work for us, supply us with incredibly cheap and abundant energy. I am talking about science and what it is capable of. It is the only thing that can bring about a utopia.

The Isociety

I am impressed sometimes with how my wishes come true. I am an at-home person. There was a time when I was starving. I thought to myself, if only I could get things from a store across the block, while the nearest store to it is far away. That and other things I am about to describe became true for me. Just in a different place from my old one. The government pays for my housing. With an EBT card I get food from a store just one block away. It is what so many desire, to have guaranteed income, which is becoming more and more of a reality. At the same time people desire to be at home more and more, and for good reason. We have more than we ever had. We need a place for it. And it takes something like a home to enjoy most of it. At home delivery of packages is evolving. You can now track the driver up until the point they arrive. And with an EBT card or regular money you can have good priced groceries sent to your home. These are some of the elements that I call an "isosociety."

It is built around what most of us want. To have the best of things around them, within their reach. To have a universal basic income. To be assured of housing. In fact buildings are more cheaply and easily made than ever, a fact which is increasing. So are our resources increasing. People fear that androids will take over our work. Fear not, that is a good thing. Things like robots, androids, and other new advancements occurring (of which there is really too much to speak of) will increase our resources and establish a low effort way of bringing to people all the things they need. As a result, universal basic income will become more and more practical. Besides, a person can do all the work they want to: *if* they want to. They can even choose exactly what that work is. They can be entirely free to pursue their dreams. They can benefit as much from them, in fact maybe even more. We need just one serious advancement to realize these dreams. Such as limitless energy. Just one thing can change the world altogether. Drones and robotics can be made to create structures. If energy is free then that is dealt with. In fact they can do so very efficiently and without resting. Just think, these buildings being created with no cost higher than the machines themselves. And– what if the machines made the machines?

The Isociety is a "society of isolation" which isn't *really* isolation. We will have technology to talk not only to our loved ones but anyone in the world itself, as is already so, only added upon. Added upon by things like holograms. Maybe we can have a camera kind of window into our loved one's home. Just think of that: visually they are always there.

Futurism

I can talk of futurism but I will leave out the dates they will occur. There is no knowing really when future things will occur. That part of it is pointless. However in doing these things I go off the rule that science and technology is capable of anything.. Sooner or later. My emphasis will be on the utopia producing sciences.

In deterring crime we could have AI cameras. Cameras that know exactly who a person is. Cameras that can track criminals from what place to another, whatever it is that they have done. These cameras do not have to be in a person's home. Personally I would include one in mine. Solid energy could create a protective field around someone. GPS enabled tags can indicate where your stolen property is, including something as important as your car. AI cameras could also spot just what someone is carrying. No longer a difficult process to determine.

The opening of resources could be greatly improved with improved metal detectors. We would then be able to determine what is in any part of the ground. Machinery can do all of that on its own. Could find and procure whatever. Being able to create the elements in a lab might be possible someday. After all, we can create diamonds. As stated before, machines can make machines that make structures and do other things. Lab grown meat might become a reality. Perhaps much quicker growing seeds too, even a food replicator such as in Star Trek. Then there could be fish catching things. Imagine a large fish-like robot that swallows just what you want to eat. Like a lobster. You throw the thing into the water and it swims all around looking for one, swallows it, and brings it back to you.

Living longer can become a thing. More and more scientists are learning what ages us and are looking into the reversal of it. More and more health improving medication is being produced as well. Emergency help will be automated. Having a device on you that knows you are having a heart problem, for example, or that you have fallen, or become lost somewhere, will be a worry of the past.

Solid energy could accomplish a number of great things. It can create walls, barriers, and imagine a glove that controls solid energy that is like a hand. Solid energy can build bridges, can create doors that just can't be broken into. It can be made into elevators. It could be incorporated into boots to walk on air. By making the solid energy go round and round, they could, perhaps, be made to function like a wheel.

Limitless energy could do incredible things for us. It could power great robotics and make any given thing automated. Such a thing would guarantee free energy for all. With energy being without limitation so too would electronics of various kinds be employed anywhere. Then there is something maybe even better: wireless energy. If you add both of them together then imagine your devices always being fully charged. Imagine posts around that charge what you need to charge. Imagine power going into anything without one plug.

AI can produce things of entertainment on its own. After that anyone can be a director. Perhaps by feeding in a script the AI will design a movie, cartoon, or game based on it. If a game then you will just carefully list what you want it to include and there it is. The program itself would basically be a book anyone can use and modify. We can bring back old stars that have passed away. We could create a new Andi Grifith series. Developed enough, computer animation will look entirely life-like. It is already becoming so that essays are being written by AI and paintings being made by them according to a few words to start it off. What power would the copyright have after that point? Where anyone can put together such things easily, and so many doing so, nothing is off the table.

Then there are driverless vehicles. At the moment they need to work some things out but they should be here before too long. What I would like is a driverless RV going all over the country!

Why go to space yourself? With VR and android-like robotics plus faster space travel (if both become a reality) then you can go to the moon in a robotic-VR fashion. That is about the way I have always thought of space travel. In the future we wouldn't even have to leave the house to do so. Add to that things like touch sensing gloves and even the ability to smell through VR and you are practically there in reality.

Drones and robotics doing our work without another human hand having to flip a burger. There was a fast food chain that recently came out with an entirely automated restaurant in fact. People fear these things saying they are taking jobs away, but with such things comes cheaper prices, prices that simply cannot be realized otherwise. I'm talking about cleaning for you– even cleaning that is exactly according to your wishes. They do all of the grocery shopping and food delivery. If you want to you could order everything online then have some machine bring it to you. But what am I saying? That is already happening.

Things that are coming about and improving include: 3D printing, goods delivery and shipping, a greatly expanded market place, automation in so many ways, fusion energy, quantum computing, better and better smartphones, driverless vehicles, AI produced artwork, full body deepfaking, digital only gaming, at home production of many different things (including books, "full band" music, notation software, game making, t shirt making, sticker making, 3D printing of action figures or whatever else, to name a few), and flying cars (if even just in a helicopter drone sort of way.)

Augmented reality is one of my favorite new things. Where at one time we only had a bulky and limited VR headset there are now "smart glasses." They look like ordinary glasses but they do so much. You can browse the web on them. You can make it *seem* like the real thing is right in front of you (a cheat when it comes to holograms) and in fact you can use them to make a 100 inch or larger screen seem to be right in front of you. With that you can have a fully loaded TV or gaming device right in front of you.

The future looks great. If we are lucky then we will be around for a long time to enjoy it.

My View on Human Rights

I think that by and large people should be left alone to do what they want to do. As long as they aren't hurting anyone but themself then let people generally be whatever way they want to be. Allowing drugs is a tricky issue. For one, people are going to do them if that is something they got themself into. However, legalizing it only makes it more widespread. I would leave such a thing off the table then. Whenever and wherever a majority of people want a certain thing then they should get it or be allowed it. So we shouldn't force diets on them. If a person wants to smoke then let them. Or if they want to vape. I think that with alcohol, tobacco, marijuana, gambling, diet, nudism, and personal preferences, people should be allowed to roam free. They shouldn't be stifled from regulation. Rather, that people are allowed to freely grow, build, and learn. It is intellectual respect when you allow others to live freely and be themselves.

It is important to identify people who are over driven towards a cause. A cause against who and what you are, when it is none of their business to begin with. These people and their beliefs against you will find ways around your rights. They will take a normal and harmless day out of your life and choose to jail you over it. Such people are fascists. It can range from minor fascism to greater fascism, and given every opportunity for growth, but that is the nature of fascism to begin with.

Whatever happened to the lifestyles that were not so confined. We aren't allotted things like a little campfire in our backyard. One where we just want to drink a little and enjoy music. The laws demand vigilance, less they are broken. They exist with absurd reasons to begin with. No one should be pressured into allowing another to just force their way in on some false pretext. People should have the right to be alone and be left alone. To exist more like a bird than a rat.

Here I will list the rights that we should have:

The right to exist like a bird and not a rat
The right to be alone and be left alone, without the littlest pressure otherwise
The right to not be harassed by propaganda. To live without it. To be without it.
The right to go against anyone who harasses us. To strictly and powerfully defend ourselves.
The right to treat like garbage anyone who treats us like garbage. The right to oppress those who would oppress us. The right to do to anyone what they do to us.
The right to never have our rights signed away– the right to not let a paper we sign take away our rights.
The right for a mentally ill person to be without harassment.
The right to whatever diet and drug we want. To smoke and drink, to gamble, whether or not anyone approves of it.
The right to be left alone in our place without the landlord coming in to inspect it or any other kind of nonsense from people.
The right to jaywalk if we know that it is safe to do so.
The right to go to Church or protest despite the virus. The right to not wear masks.
The right to not be searched without a real warrant. To not be stopped and harassed. To go about freely without people with insane reasons bothering you.
The right to have laws be limited. That only unreasonable aggression and harm rendered another without due cause is illegal.

Which spells out: to be free. Free as the wind. Free from worry. To be sure that you can go about freely day by day and not, for some dubious circumstance, be arrested.

What I would call a good person and a bad person: First, I am a highly philanthropic person. I do care about the suffering of others. I am very slow to use the word hate in my mind or think about someone so negatively to that extent. As a result I am not a bundle of hate and anger. I believe that all people deserve at least a little respect. Personally I think that the death penalty should be left up to the victim's loved ones, like their family.

I think that a part of philanthropy is justice and such things. That it is sympathy for victims and due punishment against their assailants. In fact the laws were made by philanthropists. It is for their reasons that anarchy cannot stand. They would not have either them or their loved ones harmed. So for their son's sake, their daughters, their spouse, laws must be in place.

Actually I believe that laws should be even stronger. I mean not in all cases, certainly, but certain laws are carrying too weak a consequence as far as where I live goes. People just grabbing every little thing they can and walking out of the door, for example, knowing that little punishment will be received. Worse than that are the people who just punch another for no reason whatsoever. Sometimes knocking them out. Sometimes even killing the person. These are people who treat others worse than garbage and must be very strictly dealt with.

I don't at all think that people who do drugs are bad people, not in and of itself. It is an instance where they deserve to be considered by what they go through.

We are all different. Some of us are very different from others. I believe that there should be a place for every kind of person. Whatever that is. Whoever it is you want as your company. With its own standards, rules, laws, customs, ect. We simply cannot go forward expecting everyone to be the same around everyone else as though there is some imaginary unity to be found.

But there is a whole principle to observe here. It is something that I call **The Road to Destruction:** The road to destruction is heralded by *The Principle of Convolution.* It is a theory that things become more and more convoluted over time until the bubble bursts. What were once simple laws and regulations become hardened.. Hardened like steel, a blade you could say. One that cuts deep into every aspect of life. What was once a small budget for a government becomes one greatly bloated. Not all things can be afforded after a certain point, yet the people demand they continue to be supported. Methods and means to a presumably better society are snatched up along the way. As though menial things deserve to be perfected. They don't. And you would be surprised at how well people can get by if they have to. In such a process as that, a strong person is kept weak all of their lives. The sacrifices are just considered too great, all the while. A little bit of traffic ingenuity becomes far too complicated. Laws begin to become unreasonable. The bad guy is always finding ways around them: like cheaper drugs, more easily created drugs. In so many ways criminals become smarter all the while.

And the only thing that can change everything is that moment that chaos bursts through. That is certain because things can only be kept together for so long. It is, at least, a new start. Not a start from the very bottom kind of thing. But a great time of reflection and peering into what truly worked and what didn't. To know good from bad at last. To fit everything in its proper place.

Philanthropy and Good-Heartedness is the way to go

A nation that provides for its citizens instead of running all over them will last much longer. It will thrive. Unfortunately no amount of good can deter a person whose heart has grown sour from doing wrong. The selfish heart. The life that only knows pleasure and wants more of it is a harmful presence in the world. People will amp up their power all they can by being a part of a group of people wanting the same. Wickedness grows like a monster before everyone. Then, a spark of good appears. One word, one need, one resolve to make things better. It multiplies quickly. And people who would never harm another living person simply discover that they must be as strong as they can to defeat this enemy of evil and hatred. Before then many will go their way continuing to hold out on all the hope that they can. But when people come together to bring about good in the world there is nothing that can stop them.

So when everyone is looting, do not. When everyone is rioting, don't be a part. Remain steadfast in your wholesome ways and rest your hope on the good of man coming through. It will appear mighty and strong when it comes about. Then the decrepit will change. Things will start to become better again. There are people in horrible lots. Under a government that would torture them over any resistence whatsoever. They execute out of paranoia under an evil ruler. In an idea world such states would be entirely abolished by greater powers. But that is just not possible.

Our country is full of wickedness itself. There is a side that never really sees it. They see awful things occurring on the news but do not grasp just how bad and widespread it is. So much of it does not enter into our knowledge. Too few of us really care. As long as it isn't affecting us, we think. And our sympathy might be minimal. But behind any door there can be a monster. In any heart there can be those who plot future evil, and those that see their plans through. So out of nowhere they strike. They take, they randomly damage things, and all sorts of really bad things. It is a sad reality of the world we live in.

This world is no paradise. Far from it. It is a nightmare for some. It is a sad thing for others. There is death and suffering all around at all times. Our time is coming soon itself. But when thine eyes open and see the glory of Heaven, one wonders what took them so long to get there. So rest your hope in The Lord Jesus Christ.

Finding Your Style, Personality, and Even Your New Accent

People find it difficult to just suddenly start talking in a new accent. Some find it hard to just take on a new name among people they already know. Some are even too embarrassed to accept a new name from another. But given the strength to do so you can truly find your own person. It is worth a look to see just what kind of character you are. It is something everyone does during a particular period in their lives. That is around the age of 13-20 I would put it. After that it gets dimmer and dimmer. You are just you after that, and how boring! My new personality comes on strong while I am Schizophrenic. I have a rarer symptom of it that leads me to act childishly, like an evil kid. Not even "childish" but more like a child with an adult brain (instead of pretending.) I had my own accent for a while. That itself sounded childish, and evil at the same time. I was an evil kid. But I was willing to take on any part: a news reporter, a detective, in my pretending. Sometimes I would just randomly start talking in a foreign accent as though I was possessed somehow. And I would freely dance where music was present. I was entirely uninhibited in fact. Would walk strangely, moving my arms and legs in strange ways. If I was a character I guess it would best be called "an evil kid."

Some would rather be vampires. For some it is a goth thing. For others, punk. For some metal heads. I recommend putting in your own touch instead of simply mimicking a pre-set design. Some write entire stories about characters that never existed before them. Some take an old thing and transform it based on their own interpretation. They include the things that influence them. They really enter into the world that they have established for these characters. Through my own books I am the Gray Shephard.

The More Important Things In Life

Lofty headed thinkers may lead you to believe that one must always be vigilant in not letting bad thoughts enter into your mind. Most of them are bad. So blank yourself out, is the thing they'd teach you. A little good advice can do you well. As found in a self help book with whatever thing you need help on (less worry, less complication, less bad feelings, less guilt, and so on.) I don't even need the whole book. I just found that little bit of advice I needed, something from a different perspective I wouldn't have considered otherwise. Like "stop feeling sorry for yourself." Didn't know that was what I was doing, but it was.

Some days are duds. Some days are brighter than others. We just have to accept being bored sometimes. We have to accept a lesser meal sometimes while on other days we get a fully loaded pizza. Good things come for those who wait. That's because you build up a desire for them.

We should have things to do. Humans are a being that is always on the move. Much more so than angels, trust me. So a routine is good to have. A routine is dependable. A routine organizes things. A routine is just a pleasure to have. They can include creative things, cleaning, writing, drawing, making music, self care, going somewhere once a week every week, a job, but also smaller things. Smaller things such as just making coffee for yourself in the morning. The rule is that once you are done you are done. Move on to the next thing. After all, if you finish when you still want to do more of it, your desire will be stronger for it the next time instead of burning yourself out on it.

Life is simple pleasures. To have a nice drink, nice food, good entertainment, and comfort. Comfort is a nice chair. If you are going to be sitting for any period then you should have a nice comfortable chair. Call it your throne! A chair that only you can use. Entertainment is easier to come by than ever. I was around in the days of the CRT. These fat monstrous things if you are ever going to have one 32 inches in size. Sometimes we just have to be sponges. Just taking things in knowing that there is really nothing else to do at the moment, nothing we are willing to do anyways. I like to have iced tea all day long. It is one of my pleasures in life.

It is good to have a purpose and work towards a better future. If you are to be remembered, appreciated, and have any possibility of a more significant life then daily work might be required of you. It drives me to do what I do: write. In whatever way you can, dream big and make those dreams come true. What great thing you want to be among the people is not going to be easy to come by. "Keep the faith" in these things.

One of my pleasures is to shop. It is therapeutic for many people.

We must be mature in life if things are going to go smoothly for us.

Stay away from drugs. Trust me, it isn't worth it. Flat out deny it.

Don't do any sort of thing that would put you in prison.

Get away from bad environments the best that you can.

And do not invite anyone bad into your life.

Try to enjoy simple things.

And live well.

Always.

Earth is a Prison

One in which we were made to bring about our own paradise. One in which the lesser souls were sent here early and the greater souls were sent down later. And, nearing the end of its labor: then the greater come down upon it to take it. Those that came down later were with God longer. They don't remember. You and I don't remember. That is because we were put into the flesh. Our memories became only the memories that the flesh could provide. In our early infant years we hadn't had the capacity to remember a single thing, not for long. As our brains formed, that was beyond us. The later we came upon this Earth the greater in Heaven that we were: but not always. Most of the time, but not always. For some beings it didn't matter to God what lot they would receive upon coming down. They were simple pawns sometimes sent into very bad lives. Usually they were the "hopeless" kind.

It was our labor (mostly *their* labor) to make the world what it is today. We were thrown out of paradise to make a new one. It has taken a great deal of time to get this far. But what we pose to set forth is a marvelous thing in the universe. Lately aliens (angels) have been whispering into the ears of scientists things to propel us along. God gave us all of the resources we could ever need. To take a look upon the Earth and see all of its contents and that is for sure.

The Ways of Aliens (Angels)

If they come down upon the Earth they have usually come into upper class form. They share bodies. They are astral-projectors. They fake death. They fake sleep. If they want to leave a human shell they just make themselves have a heart attack. All that Earth sees is the dead body of a familiar person. The soul then goes where it will. Back above or into some other body. They pretend to sleep. They don't want it to look like they are inhuman after all. While they are laying down with their eyes closed they leave their bodies and go where they need to go. They can go across the globe instantly if they want to. After their work is done they enter into the body of a wealthy person. The angel that previously inhabited that body might go back to work or whatever else. That is their reward and their vacation. Some of them are there to slip in knowledge, some are there to stabilize things, some are protecting important people, and some are there to simply observe us. If they have to fell a human being they do it from a distance. They "will" that the person dies in any sensible way. Like if they are known to have heart problems they render them a heart attack. Those are usually people harmful towards God's purpose. They could just be a person that is harmful towards proper human evolution and His desired course of things.

So when a person of importance is walking down the street in a bad area, you can be assured that there are angels there looking on. Through a door or something, through a window, being able to see and sense things better. What bad things are very likely otherwise are prevented. Such a person can even miraculously seem to survive the worst of things.

Then sometimes it is like a chess game between good and iniquity. From which entire new religions are formed to counter another. It was more a thing of the past when angels would suddenly appear before a human being and before you know it a "divine revelation" was revealed. Obviously such things are not so easy to secretly pull off.

Some Ideas on a New Church

I would have to go against a typical design since what I offer is not typical. I would say a good Church has its members creating things. Things that further the Church itself and the religion that it teaches. In that, those who would create good things (determined to be worth it) should be given what they need to do so and some sort of avenue to "get it out there." If they are really good at writing, painting, writing music, or creating whatever, then the best thing to do is to give them the sorts of things they need to create. For example a word processor for authors, a canvas and paint for artists. Their reward is keeping those things. If their heart is in it then they will continue to work with those things.

I think there should be a subset of interests present. In other words not just religious teachings but a separate lifestyle found within too. Such as a retro gaming community within the church. Or a book club or whatever else. This would have to be limited, however. It would bring more people in but isn't a thing that should be watered down. So one or maybe two sub communities within every particular church.

There are some of the typical things: music, preaching, celebrating, group study, tithing, and so on.

I think that a Christian Satanic Church could really stand out. Could garner a lot of attention, good and bad (and any publicity is good publicity.) As such the Church would bear both angelic and demonic imagery. Could be three parts: one side for Christians, another for Satanists, and in the middle the "gray" area. In all things a version for each. One for hymns, another for metal, and the music you could say is in the middle of it. Remember that all of my books are free and in the public domain.

It could be a place of practicing and learning magic. Could be a place of teaching helpful things. Could be that sometimes you all go to a special place in town. People could gather to create things that would help the Church and its religions. I used to be a part of a PSR (psycho-social rehabilitation) group. These were the sorts of things we did. We had our little chores and creative classes, would go out into town sometimes, and it was all a lot of fun.

How about an old idea of mine? First, let's give it a ridiculous name. After all, everyone who makes a Church is always trying to come up with some clever crap. We'll call it "The Church of Lucifer Message In Or On Something." Its ways are simple. The members promise to leave messages about their religion and its beliefs all over the place. Slip a note into a book. Put them in a plastic bottle and put that bottle somewhere. Regularly place messages online. Just short stuff. Hand out messages too, these little books you make. Include a neat thing within your messages like a neat stone or old coin. Some stickers maybe. Make stickers that have messages on them and stick them on things.

It could also be more traveling based. Little is known about it, but there are groups that travel all over and share the expenses. If you are willing to live a simple life then that might even be a cool thing to get into or create. They have just what they need: tents, could be an RV I guess, whatever works. To make soups and simple food. To include a belly dancer, a night time fire, and just socializing with one another, are some such ideas for that.

The Childish Aesthetic

Adults can be so dull. A bedroom usually goes like this: this is where the bed goes, the TV goes here, books are stored there. With nothing ever different. Nothing ever cool. Nothing ever out of the ordinary. Yet we have invented so many cool things! We have bubble makers, fog machines, all the different kinds of lights you can imagine, to say the least. I imagine a kingdom not paved by gold but paved with board game pieces and candy. I imagine business signs being far larger, brighter, shining, with images going over them. I imagine a spot with tall adult swings just because those would be nice to swing on a while. Then after you are done shopping at the mall you can just jump down to the bottom because there is an inflated platform there.

It would be a world where things along the road are more dazzling. Where tunnels full of great lights are there just because those are cool to have. Where while passing by, billboards show awesome things. With the right to place stickers wherever you want to, and the walls are covered with them. Where you get a free glowstick just for shopping at some place. Where while drinking coffee at a coffee place the lights go off to have more brilliant and dazzling lights instead. That alongside poppy and fun music.

The sky would let forth balloons. The sky would have nighttime drones producing images. It doesn't even have to be a holiday when it happens. Things would be less plain. Things will all be more artistic and unique from one to another. At least it could be a little more like *Blade Runner*. Windows would more often be more stained glass. Wall paper would be prominent over just painted walls. Walls would go beyond the white. Digital picture frames would replace static ones on the walls, containing a person's favorite images. You could dress however you want to. You could dress and go about like an animal of your choice.

It would be common to find things like mood rings, punch balloons, pogs, toy musical instruments, colorful marbles, twelve sided dice, token coins, and even more expensive things like little game machines, on the ground. With the right to "litter" such stuff that can happen!

Fast food places would have signs that go high and are much larger. It could be like a star with digital images flashing across it and on the hour it plays "twinkle twinkle little star" and winks at you. Things like beaded doorways, haphazard arcade machines, token and games, vending machines, carnival game areas, neon colors, things that glow in the dark, and friendship bracelets, would become more common. Special lights can go a long way as well. Such lights that we have that we never use. Again, adults are a boring, dead, and plain lot. What about using LEDs, black lights, glow fluid, strobe lights, neon lights, projectors, lasers, more often?

Those are the things I would bring about, but it would take me being like a King to make it happen, which isn't going to happen.

Being the Devil's Child is Being the Devil's Kid

Let's not mistake being Satan's kid with being God's child. One is disciplinary and strict. The other spoils us. Unlike God, Satan wants us to be greedy and selfish. He wants us to act like a child. After all, when reading all this that Paul wrote and going over things like the Proverbs, you can be sure that most Satanists are getting it wrong. They mistakenly replace what God does with what Satan is. Many Satanists are coming off of the Christian doctrine and have unfortunately found a sort of evil Father in Satan. He would have us be less inhibited. More self seeking. More pleasure finding. More worldly. That is a key thing about Satanism: worldliness.

Satanists do not consider the reversal of Christianity enough. If it is to be a reversal then there is a lot to go over. Unfortunately Satanists are limited in their scope while doing so, if they do at all. Let us remember Satan's other traits as well. Those traits that not enough of us ever consider. Like the fact that Satan is *subtle* and so be subtle. He represents perfection, the height of music, as well as individuality and rebellion. He himself was like a spoiled child. The whole fact is that pop music is more Satanic than metal music.

Being Poorly Guided

I tell you that it is a cult that Anton LaVey has put upon his followers. His followers worship him in every way. That "great leader" that "revolutionary thinker" is no different than any other cult leader. As well it is a religion that isolates its followers. It does so in an innovative way: by making isolation seem like a quality lifestyle choice. Like any other cult it holds a monopoly on what it is. No other religious beliefs can be mixed in. Just like a cult it is constricting. Just like any other cult it leads you to believe that its followers are changing the entire world. That what they do is amazing. That "thank God you found us and became a part of us!"

But it is all just a lot of nonsense. When I hear Anton LaVey speaking I only hear a guy with a shy guilty voice knowing exactly what he was doing, in a "just make up nonsense with big words" sort of way. His followers can never shut up about him. They don't realize that the power to just live has been taken from them. And it is a religion that has made virtually no impact on the world. It never was a successful thing. They say "we've been around for 40 years" but in what way? I don't ever even hear of these people besides some lame documentary or one of their brainwashed followers getting onto YouTube.

They say such strange things, too. Often things that don't make sense or things built around what their leader would say. He mentioned werewolves and not vampires so they like the werewolf more and are ready to speak on that.

If you are caught up in all of it I only ask from you that you consider for a moment if you are being taken advantage of or not. If you can live without the words of this man, or if you are captivated by it all for some strange reason. Unfortunately, in most cases, there is no talking someone out of a cult.

But here is the most powerful cult that has ever been: the cult of modern society, which is especially strong in American life. They would have you think, act, and speak only according to them. If you stray for a moment in thought, you could say something that costs you your career and livelihood. There are all kinds of terms thrown in. Just like a cult! A cult has words for ideas like that– for concepts, convenient words used to ostracize you. They have stifled a precious thing: free thought. There are different kinds of cults, cults that are different sometimes, and sometimes just different branches of the same thing. Another one is made up of conspiracy people fanatics. They are downright Schizophrenic without actually being that way. They think things I would only think while unmedicated. Unlike me though they continue to function somehow.

Demons have poured over upon the face of the Earth. The abyss has been opened. Abaddon and his might appears. And people are being separated into two classes: the good and the faulty. Those that are blameless, mature, and do well in life. Then there are those that break out in demon speak, appearing demon possessed because they are. The good people will be the only ones to see the end of it all. There has become a great big mess for the aliens and humans to deal with and sort out, but it is a necessary thing.

Be guided into good deeds even when it is hard to do so. Keep faith in the good. It could come at quite a high price to make one wrong choice. Just smile and know that the bad people will soon be met with a harsh fate. Eventually a bad acting person is going to become so bad that they'll be punished for it. In the meantime they are oblivious to that fact. So when a guy spontaneously yells at you just know he is going to do so elsewhere, again and again until he takes things too far and must pay the price. Do not go along with them. Don't do the dance with them. Be different. Be like a person walking in the lion's den. They are like people looking for an excuse. That would say anything they can to rouse you enough to punch them, and then Karen yells "assault!" But go along with the rules and do right and the judge will not see any wrong in you.

As for me I am without friends: just as I want it to be. I can't imagine having a good time at someone else's house. That's just the way I am. Nor can I stand anyone in my house other than me. I have my own things to do when I want to do them. It has always served me well, too. The only people I ever speak to are my family and that is just letters, gifts, and texts. It's enough for me. Most problems arise from groups. Without a group there are no gangs. Without a harmful group there is no inspiration. Without a religious group there is no spiritual-genocide.

Some Anti-Cult Rules

It isn't too hard at all to come up with rules that would prevent a religion from becoming one. Cults depend on just a few things and those things are as fully implemented as possible, but are only a few. These could also reveal to you if you are in a cult or not.

Isolation- They bring about seclusion from non members. They make you hate the world and the people within it. They make others seem like bad people that you should have nothing to do with. They teach that only they should teach you, having the only source of heightened knowledge.

Exemplification- They make their leader seem god-like. They make him or her seem like they were the smartest thing to ever come forth from humanity. That only their leader can impart the greatest knowledge. Usually a person of a profound past. Someone with just the right circumstances in place to have learned or discovered what they did.

Give-All- They'll rob you blind. They will take every bit of money you have. They'd have you sell your properties. They would take everything from you.

Monopoly- They are the only right religion. They are the only ones of the truth. They are the only right way. They are those that left a different religion to find the new one through their great leader. Anyone who modifies their beliefs in any way are liars and frauds. They are the enemy.

Greatness- They will lead you down the true path in life. Through them and only them does one evolve. Only they can offer such a thing. Only they can lead you into Heaven. Only they can teach you the things you need to transcend.

There was a time when I was in a hotel. I didn't have the kind of money to stay there for very long. I had just until next morning to leave. So I was looking for some sort of shared housing to get. I had received a paper just for that. One I got in jail before I was released. I used to walk, like crazy long distances. After hours of walking I came upon the home that was listed. Some sort of Christian home that didn't seem so bad. But the moment they asked for my phone, my SSI payment card, and to be searched for anything additional not allowed in this "holy" place, I left. The moment they left the room I said "nope!" and I walked out the door.

A Message to My Followers

Your wellness is important to me. I have always sought to unselfishly make you the best people you can be. I am not here to take a single thing from you. I am only here to add to the quality of your life and create a thing that only I can create. Through the purpose given to and that I have given myself it might not even be any mistake that you have found me. Over the years I have dealt with a lot. I have put a lot of my personal faith upon the future of these things. My life can be so fragile. I am bound with medication that if I didn't have it I would literally go insane. That so often leads to jail time for me. Mental hospitals and things. I have been homeless before. So I write now so that at least I have my message to bring others online even at times when I am not before a computer.

I am not interested in money. I have the money I need apart from all of this. In fact my books are set at zero revenue because I don't need that money and would rather have my paperback books be as cheap as possible. My books are all in the public domain too. Of which I have written nearly 60 books at this time. I am doing what I was meant to do. That doesn't make me special or anything. I as well encourage you and anyone to form new religions on what I have done, wherever they are similar or not is up to the designer. I am more a person of ideas. Ideas that can be used, useful ideas. I am more the start of a thing then the completion and fullness of it because I believe that my followers should be able to create their own from what I have presented.

I am not a pervert either. I am not after anything sexual. I am not some creep with a bent mind control cult. I am in fact largely asexual, especially in these years of mine. I do not like it when things are sexualized or the people who do that.

You can trust me. You can depend on me. I however am not in any way a public spokesperson. I wouldn't be a part of any interview. If a publisher wanted to publish any of my books I would just say "just do it, it is in the public domain though." My ebooks are all free. Naturally I cannot make the paper based books free. I hand them out if a friend seems interested. I never read my own writings. I am not even invested in an egotistical way. Offered power, I would decline. There is nothing in that for me. That is just a lot of work with a result I don't need. Control people to do what? I never understood why people want power to begin with. Power just corrupts them all too well and leads them into punishment.

Rather I write because I know that certain forces expect it of me. The more I write and continue to write, the better my life will be. Let me tell you the one thing I do want: it is fame. Fame enough to go online and see myself being discussed and maybe the more significant kind of life that comes from that. To be someone, this lonely person that I am.

I have hear a list of music videos for my beloved followers:

The Cranberries: Dreams
Poppy: Bleach Blond Baby
Pat Benatar: We Belong
Sneaker Pimps: Six Underground
Legend (Tangerine Dream)- Loved By The Sun
Live: I Alone
Bjork: Human Behavior
Black Sabbath: N.I.B.
Samael: Rebellion
Samael: Slavocracy
Enigma: The Child In Us
Legend: Lily's Dark Dance
Sixpence: Don't Dream It's Over
Final Fantasy 8: "The Ending"
Sting: If I Ever Lose My Faith In You
Grimes: Player Of Games
Final Fantasy 9- Melodies of Life
Enigma: Sadness
Madonna: Ray of Light
Poppy: Fill The Crown
Aqua: Good Morning Sunshine
The Police: Wrapped Around Your Finger
Mono: Life In Mono
Rihanna: Diamonds
Juliana Hatefield: Witches Song
Alison Krauss: When You Say Nothing At All
Shawn Covlin: Sunny Came Home
Madonna: Don't Cry For Me Argentina
Jewel: Hands
Pretenders: Don't Get Me Wrong
Queen: One Vision

Finding and Making the Right Home

Some are religious based, a type that has long been around. Some are government run like the SRO that I live in. There are helpful staff here. Then there are nursing homes, work based living circumstances, the boarding care, the group home, the shelter, the low income house, the section 9 homes, temporary living, a vacation home, RV lots, and more. I think a cool idea is having a hotel subscription going from hotel to hotel while traveling around the country. Some are campers. They move to new spots to any new place they are allowed to camp.

In the future homes will be more easily come by. People could pretty much be guaranteed a home before too long. That is because making homes is becoming easier all the time, even if they are just mini types of homes with the most basic of things: water and power. When it comes about that we find a cheaper and more abundant form of energy then this will just speed up greatly.

The cheaper forms of living include any place that houses the low income. RVs too, which are rather cheap and usually include things like power, water, and cable. Trailers are normally cheaper. I had an uncle that stuck two of them together in a very small community of people in the Arizona desert. We had water at least, though no hot water. I had an aunt that literally lived in the desert in a small trailer. I have had to live with roommates before, the kind in the same room as me. I can tolerate nearly any home condition except for that. Being in a hotel with thin walls, you can get some noise coming through. My solution was a fan-sound white noise machine, and it blocks out all outside noise surprisingly well. As much as the moment I turn it off yelling is clearly heard. Fortunately it is the type of sound (the fan sound) that I don't have to pay attention to.

In certain countries living in tiny rooms is a thing. You barely have room in them for anything. I guess that is either okay or not based on the kind of person you are. My room isn't at all large. I have a lot of tables, large storage containers, and such things to store my things. It doesn't look like hoarding if things are stored away. Instead of people seeing things all over the place they just see storage containers stacked up. The worst thing I have encountered in a home was mushrooms growing out of the carpet. Also a toilet in a shack I lived in led to a broken sewer that puddled up outside. Then the people that ran the boarding care I was once in were strict as hell. Always cleaning up our messes with every bit of complaints they could make against it. That place closed down.

If I had a dream home it would be more than a home: a palace. My dream palace would contain five sections: The Master of Expression Section, The Taste Section, The Memory Section, The Magic Section, and The Glow In The Dark House. The master of expression section would contain everything I need to express myself. The taste section has every bit of good food there is to have. The memory section would contain the things of my memory, nostalgia. The magic section would have everything I need to practice magic. Then the glow and the dark house in the center, which is where I can have comfort and entertainment. In my days of grandiosity that was a dream of mine. I wouldn't have a white home or a black home, I would have mine glow in the dark. And I would make it where I could sleep on the roof with a blanket, looking up at the stars. In fact at times when I had enough privacy I didn't wear clothing in my room beyond a comforter blanket to wrap around me.

Not cleaning shows low functionality, a type of depression, and at worst feelings of being meaningless. It can take an awful lot for some people to clean their home. For some it just doesn't work right. There are things to make it easier though. To have carpet you can easily vacuum and a nice vacuum. To only have as many dishes as you need at any given time so they don't pile up. Don't think that giving chores to your kids is a bad thing. It teaches them to work and that is a very important lesson in life. They might even clean their own home up someday. I used to be a messy person until I went into some group homes that required me to do chores. Now cleaning it along the way is just natural for me. What once felt like work no longer does. If I want it super clean then I spend a few hours on it, this little room.

Best of all, a home is a place for your neat things. I most recently got a thermal printer and 500 sheets of paper for it. Such a cheap way of making any black and white sticker. That is a kind of thing I like to make, stickers. The thing prints instantly too. The paper is dirt cheap. It's awesome. I have gratitude for all I have. That is a good form of therapy, going over all you have and being thankful for it. It brings greater appreciation after all. I have all I need to write, for my prayer sheets, and those unusual things I do. I have a large powerful fan for the hotter days, which, in San Francisco, that's all you need. I've got an excellent ice making machine. I have a deep freezer. I have a coffee machine that both grinds and brews coffee. The more normal things: a regular printer, microwave, tables, shelves. I have a thick 100 percent cotton blanket and a polyester comforter. I have four pillows and want five. A moon chair, which is like half of a tilted sphere. When I write I like to put on my expensive gold rings. I want to get a digital picture frame just to have my favorite images (which to me are like idols) displayed on it. I have two temperature gauges. During the back-to-school days I grab a ton of paper notebooks. They are just something like 30 cents at the time, so I might grab nearly a hundred of them. I think what I have more than anything else as far as one kind of thing goes are pens. I could fill buckets with how many I have. All of different styles, different colors, some more like markers, others ballpoint, and I don't know how it came to be that I would have so many. I like having them though. I write on the walls too, basically. I have dry erase boards all over.

Inflation? Bah! I don't believe in inflation. Things are becoming both cheaper and better all the time. There was a time when an underdeveloped computer cost an arm and a leg. My little smart phone is many times more powerful than that and didn't even cost much. Certain things that I once could only dream about having in my home are now here and were not hard to come by. For example, at one time all I could have for a big TV was a costly 32 inch CRT TV. The thing was a monster in weight and bulkiness. Then recently I bought a 43 inch flatscreen Samsung (great brand) Smart TV. Something that at one time would have cost far more. When flat screens were coming out, having a small one was all you could afford. Less components and lighter weight after all, cheaper to make, cheaper to ship. Not to mention augmented reality that produces a very large screen right before your eyes. (Even cheaper, smaller, more lightweight.) Then there is cable TV which is becoming obsolete. Roku and other streaming things do it better and for free. There are many such examples of this but I'll spare you the details. They have said in the recent past that the economy was in shambles but I sure see people packing into fast food places.

A home is your own place. It is a place where you gather the best things which in today's time there is no lack of. It might be a place where you creatively work. Or sometimes just a place where you sit for a long movie and a few shows. Hopefully you have the food, water, energy, comfort, and entertainment you need.

The Lighter, Darker, and Gray Side To Things

Find the light to be positive. It is the brighter side of things. It is the yin. The darker side is the negative. It is the darker, the obscure. It is the yang. The gray side is the hidden side, the shadowy, obscure, in a place in between. It is the invisible circle around the yin yang. In fact a better yin yang symbol would contain a gray circle around it.

The lighter side of life is found in its happier times. The darker side is in its sadder times. The gray side is during the more meditative states that we have.

The lighter side of relationships is when things go well. It is in those moments where we truly love our partner. The darker side is in its arguments. The gray side to it is the times when you are just peacefully watching a movie together.

The lighter side of days are those days you are happily on vacation. The darker side of days are those days you might be in jail, or any bad place. The gray side of days are those days where you are peacefully creating something.

The lighter side of the world are those parts where happiness and freedom abound. The darker side are those places where evil rules. The gray parts are those places just being built and have not really yet begun.

The lighter side of jobs are those times when things are going quickly and smoothly. The dark side to jobs are when your boss mistreats and even belittles you. The gray side is when you are on break.

The lighter side of creating is when you are proud of what you are doing. The darker side of creating is when you have no idea what you are doing. The gray side of creating is when things are pretty much automatically being done, such as auto writing.

The lighter side of groups is the party and personal pleasure without harm alongside it. The darker side is when you are attacked by one. The gray side is when you want to be with it, but not totally.

The lighter side of shopping is when you find the exact thing that you want. The darker side is the long line at the checkout. The gray side is when you peacefully stroke the isles finding what you want, though not immediately sure.

The lighter side of laws is that things are kept in order and your life might have even been saved. The darker side of them is when you are blamed and lied about in order to be punished. The gray side is when things might be made more complicated by them, but perhaps worth it.

The lighter side of pleasure is the joy it brings. The darker side is when a negative side effect comes about or even a bad overdose. The gray side is waiting for it to arrive.

The lighter side of family is that you have a legacy. The darker side of a family is a drunk father. The gray side of a family is one you don't really care about, but you don't not care about them either.

The lighter side of health is that you will live long with a good diet and exercise. The darker side to health is that to be healthy requires diet and exercise. The gray side of health is when you find an acceptable balance.

The lighter side of roommates is that they help with the rent. The darker side is that they are annoying or don't cover their costs. The gray side is that they cover most of the rent but not all of it, and are only somewhat a nuisance.

The lighter side of religion is that you have a group to grow with in neat and interesting ways. The darker side is when you all kill yourselves, as you are in a cult. The gray side is when you want to be a part but the sermon can be a bit boring.

The lighter side of vacation is when you are there and finally find your fun and relaxation. The darker side of a vacation is the time it takes to get there. The gray side of it is in the bittersweet end. You have just a little more to enjoy. So you must make the best of it.

My Philosophy On Making A Good Video Game

I adore the retro gaming community. It is rather large. It composes a lot of what videos are placed online and I always enjoy watching them. In my darker times I had at least the thoughts of old games and enjoyed thinking about them, whatever I could remember. Getting my freedom and home back I watched retro gaming videos more than anything else. That is where my experience comes from. I always wanted to program a game. Even got a bit into python. I came to a point where I decided I would be a writer and nothing else. Everything else was just a short lived thing. I have electronic components I will probably never use. I have switches of all kinds, small solar panels, a soldering iron, bread boards, and so on. There was a time when making a video game controller and machine was something I wanted to do, but at the time there was no practical way. Then 3D printers and things like mini computers came along. By then though I lost interest in making such a thing.

What I can do however is provide ideas. That is just as important as the programming itself. So many people immediately think that making a game means programming and nothing else. They then won't get involved in the process because they think that's all it means. No, though, producing ideas and such things is just as important. I have made a few video game idea books. The Game Makers Bible, The New Video Game Idea Book, Making A Great Game, New Video Game Ideas, and New Ideas For Video Game Things. Those are under my birth name: Adam Jeremy Capps. Then there is my Antichrist Game or Movie book under my name Lucifer Jeremy White which is largely about making a Satanic video game. Like all of my books they are free (as ebooks) and in the public domain.

To briefly go over what makes a good game:

1– The mechanics have to be so that the character is easy to control. That is the very basis of the game, after all. The better it is to control the character the better they can do every other little thing.

2– When a game is cloned it only looks like an ugly cousin. The gamer thinks that it only looks like an ugly version of something else. The better games started off as their own things instead of a copy of something else. I wouldn't include contrasts like Street Fighter to Mortal Kombat, however, which were done so differently.

3– Amusement. There is the idea that people like cartoons. Cartoons that can be totally against any possible reality. Yet when it comes to making games game companies believe it should all be as much a movie as possible. More and more game making companies are making things as realistic as possible. But the Mushroom Kingdom still stands strong.

4– Fun. A good game is fun. Some build their entire basis around that. "Is it fun?"

5– Is not rushed. Is instead well polished. The little details are gone over and improved. Things that simply won't work are tossed aside. Is not overworked in the wrong areas however, with the things that mean the least left alone, instead to focus on the more important aspects. There is the story of the painter who painted over his original painting so much that it became a big unrecognizable mess.

6– Give the players what they want. Have many options. Make it flexible. Have it contain different paths, different ways to play, since not every gamer wants the same thing.

7– Make it easy to grasp. Make it easy enough to understand. Don't leave the player with the burden of figuring things out and never really getting it. Wherever you can simplify something, do so. The goal is to make it natural and intuitive for the player.

9– Make it engaging. Especially in certain genres like the RPG. A good story is of utmost importance in an RPG. Split people up to make the best story they can. Then bring it together into one. Bring the player into the journey.

10– Good music is very important. Look for the best composer you can without settling until you find the best. Inspiration from old classical music is common. Things beyond any copyright, but done in the composer's more desirable way.

11- Don't start with an empty slate. Don't jump from a little paperwork on it to starting the whole process of making it. First, create every little idea of what you want done. Share things with your team. Make it a good collaboration. Complete any drawings you need. When you have brought together a lot of good ideas then you can start to actually make the game.

12– Find inspiration. I have seen again and again a game making company wanting a game like one or another only in a better way: a better version of something before it. The best ones were not so much a copy. Sometimes they are a totally superior thing. And sometimes they just returned to an old idea making it so much better that it became one of the greatest games ever. Such as with the original Mega Man, which was a flop, but Mega Man 2 was the start of a great and long running franchise. The kind of inspiration I am talking about can be compared to how Ninja Gaiden was inspired by Castlevania.

13– Remember that what works works and in some cases just doesn't need any improvement or difference to it. Such as the idea that so many love to this day: random and turn based battles. Or the concept of in game money. There are certain things that are great and cannot do any better. Changing them can in fact be a bad thing so they are best left as-are.

14– Look for that great new idea. Add great new ideas upon great new ideas. In the gaming world there are copy cats and those that truly progress things. When Mario Bros. came out so many games followed suit. They were barely as good as Mario with little innovation to the idea. Then Mario Bros. 3 came out. That is the way that Mario should have inspired a new game from a different company, but fell very far short of it.

15– Don't give up until your best has been done. You might even reach out to see if your game meets with people's approval and seek out suggestions to make it better. When John Madden's NFL games were being made they presented the result to Madden to see if he approved of it or not. He immediately told them: "there are not enough players on the field!" That must have been good advice as it went on to be the most successful of NFL video game franchises.

Why I Am Not Into Relationships, "Friends," Or Even Company

The person who is never lonely exists. I am him. I spend my days happy and alone with never another soul in my room. I am beyond any understanding of why people find being around others tasteful. While my siblings strive to start a family of their own there is nothing that I could desire less. I don't want a person in my room. I don't want some such person to talk to. I don't want marriage and I certainly don't want kids. I think I am better off without them saving all my time for myself. I will never have the responsibility required of raising a child. Will never have to buy them clothing and food with my money. All of my money will always be for myself. I don't have to upkeep a good home, one that stays clean, one that has high energy bills and so on.

I don't see why it isn't a choice that most people make. To me raising a child until they are 18 or beyond is a lot of work that I would never want. My books are my children. It is a thing that authors have said before me, in fact. My books say exactly what I want them to say. They grow as I want them to. They preserve who I am. They represent me, and so on.

The most contact I make with others, besides the time I have to like with the bankers, is by sending over gifts to my family. I am always happy to mail them birthday and holiday things. Especially toys to my nieces and nephews because of a concept that I like. That what I give them will be around for the next hundred years, potentially longer than that. The action figure I give will have a long life beyond me and them. Exchanging hands over time. Sold to one in the store and to another online. Possibly sought out as a treasure by someone or another. So those are the kinds of toys that I give. Some of that with the older members of my family too, only not things that are toys.

But if you ask me, I would prefer no one to be around except my family. I used to have the grandiose idea that only my family and I would be left on Earth someday, as well as a spouse for me. Just think. An Earth all for you. To the furthest reaches. That aliens came down upon Earth and removed everyone except for them. How would you spend the first week after such an event? You could loot anything you wanted to. It is now all yours completely. So after going to a big store what would be the things you take? I guess a good place to start is in the clothing area. Try out new jeans, shirt, and a jacket right there inside the store without a soul around to stop you. Putting on new socks and a nice belt. Then just take one of their bags, hell, take a cart or a rolling luggage thing they have. Put anything you want into it. Grab some food including some non-perishable stuff.

I guess you would have to look for stuff such as solar panels and gas generators. You might not have active internet for very long but there are always hard drives and memory cards, CDs, DVDs, and a ton of other ways to get all of the entertainment things you could possibly need. As for gas and propane that stuff would be in millions of vehicles, vehicles which you can pick from and take. What vehicle would you grab? Let's assume the people left naked. Car keys would be all over the place. Then you've got to choose what home you would be in. You could each have your own home if you wanted. To me these things would be the dream of all dreams.

No Life Is Perfectly Lived

That's why no one is really any better than the other. That is, except for truly horrible people. They may have had a rocky past and their reasons, however. But sometimes trash *is* born upon this Earth which does not belong. We all have our dumb little problems. Some are better off than others. I cannot imagine why a person would ever take their lives. I sympathize but those feelings are foreign to me. Some people have just a little bit of problems. They might be well off for most part but are worry warts, or over stressed, easily agitated. Things in your teenage years are at their worst. Always trying to fit in, the very nightmare of getting acne. That you have this cowlick on your hair that a full can of hairspray cannot fix. You start to look for inspiration. You want to be a vampire or something. I didn't find maturity until I turned 40 years old. I did though. It takes a lot to anger me. It takes a lot more for me to negatively act out on it. I would just like to peacefully go back and forth in life without being bothered. If I am bothered then as soon as I get back in my room I don't let it get to me. I've got a life to live. Personally I detest the feeling of anger. It is like emotional pain.

At least I can say that I would never do the sort of things that would put me in prison. At worst I might be charged with some dumb misdemeanor over some dumb law. There are people that are in prison for life. What a screwed up lot for them. I have been homeless but dealt with it well. It helps when you are crazy enough. Some people have been homeless for ten years, or even most of their lives.

We are all in the same boat. It isn't an easy existence. I would say it is easy enough for me. It is a strange world. We could be at our best only to suddenly get cancer or something. Some heart problems. Then before we know it we are packing our bags. If we can get by without hurting others, then great! If we can be good towards one another and not get ourselves into trouble then that is as good as it gets.

If you take into account a person's reasons, no one is ever to blame really. They had poor influences over them. Influences they could not escape or refuse. Their bread and butter and life itself just dictated certain things to them. That along with abuse from friends and family lead them to become what they became. Maybe there was something wrong with their brains, biologically.

Entering into Heaven is like opening one's eyes after a long rest. It is to see again, after being muffled, after being blind for so long. It is the sudden overwhelming feeling of peace. It is to be brought up by God from a pit. Yet we fight every day to live. We fight tooth and nail to preserve life. We are confused by its mystery. We fear the unknown. But I tell you, that once it happens, you will be happy that it didn't take any longer than it did.

Until then, live well. Be forgiving. Do not stab a knife directly in your heart, but instead understand that you are an eternal being loved by God. Be thankful that every passing day brings you closer to Heaven. One in which you will see your loved ones again, perhaps those who have been there awhile. They will have nothing but love for you, and you them. Things will have changed to the better without ever having to venture into an evil place again. In making life better, it is better that you understand these things.

Disconnecting From Popular Mindsets

Most people cannot be without problems. They cannot be without a cause which is to really say they cannot be without an enemy. They've all got to gather against certain things and share a power over it. That's so whether or not they are actually problems for any of them, personally. It is considered a glorious day for them to encounter and destroy their enemy, which comes from ideological sources. So they all strum the same tune until the next great one comes along.

Their minds are already made up for them. They have been put together by one another who share the same thoughts and purposes in life. It gives them reason for being and things to hate. The solution from them is never gentle. It is never a peaceful answer but a strict and vicious one. They seek "justice" to be the executor without any alternative answers to "their" problems.

In fact they make up many books, many documentaries, much music, almost all of the news, and groups, and things practically religions, or at least cults. To me such a thing would be an overwhelming burden, but I have a soul to begin with. These are more zombie-like people. I wouldn't lift a finger to fix their problems and they hate me for it. They depend on large numbers.

My religion is a thing made to separate myself from it and to help others separate from it. So long as we tell them that we are a part of something else (certainly something more meaningful and worthwhile) maybe they will leave us alone. Freedom of religion still exists, doesn't it? Then let us hide within ourselves with these texts guarding us. They've got no right to separate you from what *you* want to be a part of or from those who would share it with you.. Unhampered, untainted, and not blemished by them.

We will keep ourselves well enough for God and continue to learn from His wisdom. These are a people of wickedness and the very reason why society is collapsing. We will live right: without harming others, without being a problem to anyone. We will learn things such as maturity together, and we will help each other out (those among our own.) We will be a Holy Ship against the rough tides of The Tribulation. We will make from none an enemy, not even The Devil. *Especially* not him. At the same time not be a cult. With those willing and able in reasonable ways, not like in cult strictness, not separated from our family, not mistreated, not misguided. For the days ahead are rough ones. The world is overridden with wickedness. It is foolish to think that the world can do well without God and His wisdom in it. Yet we are a gray lot and are able to keep things together accordingly.

The Gray: understanding, flexible, versatile, advantageous, broader, more moderate and balanced, more fully developed, the princes and the princesses of the universe, to whom it always belonged! Not frightful Christians, not "evil" Satanists, not negligent Budhists, but of all good things brought together into one.

The Growing Monster

If today's time was a living idol it would be the most grotesque thing. It would be a slobbering behemoth. It would have hateful starry eyes. It would have vicious grinding teeth. It would have tightly clutching hands. It's heart would be hard and angry. It would be eager to kick things out of its way. It would be founded on furry. The people have risen up such a monster. Have fed it, whose appetite is never full, always wanting more. They have honored it as their own even though they should be ashamed of it and have it removed from them. It is a reflection of them.

It will only grow in power. It will destroy its own. The people would look for every way to destroy it. Will find the most potent weapon against it as possible. They will use means that only the lost would use. They will try to make it nicer and fail. They will try to change it into something pleasant, something genial, but will fail. The price of their sins will show, and even at the cost of death people will not let go.

My Panic Attacks

There are no thoughts scarier than those that I experience during a panic attack. Fortunately they have only happened to me at night time. I can depend on them not coming about during the day. They are the most horrible of feelings. I imagine *what if I was made into a cockroach?* And I imagine what a horrible thing that must be. I put myself into that perspective so literally that it scares me. Then there is the thought *someday I will die. There is no avoiding it.* That any night at all that I fall asleep I might not wake up. Maybe worst of all are those feelings of losing my mind. I am able to send my mind to scary and lost places. The fear of not emerging from it is awfully scary. It is impulsive. It forces itself upon me while it is happening. I cannot simply ignore it. All of a sudden my heart will flush with a feeling of doom coming over me. I believe I have made progress against it last night however, keeping the fact in mind that "what goes up must come down," which to me means there is no thinking yourself into death or permanent insanity. Knowing that alone is very helpful.

Materialism

Whoever first said "money can't buy you happiness" must have come from a long lost time. A time when people still didn't have much. A time when things like the park and insignificant things still mattered the most. Things have changed. There are so many good things out there to snatch up. Things that make life easier, more entertaining, happier, better. With the internet we can get just about anything we want. We can be specific. We can get things from our childhood that are otherwise lost forever.

Without certain things we can be miserable. Without those things we have become accustomed to we can be very bored. Without a little heater we can be too cold to tolerate or the same in hot weather without an air conditioner. Without morning coffee we can be irritable. We have things that suit our every hobby. If that is making music then there is notation software, keyboards, newer electronic devices, and so on. I lived in a time when my writing was limited to mechanical keyboards. Later I got a digital hybrid kind. Then I finally got Windows 95, and had a word processor which was amazing to me at the time. I am on Windows 11 currently and am quite grateful for the online publishing of books. Sometimes I think of getting a 3D printer. Those seem so cool.

There is no telling what is around the corner and it is only natural to be curious. For me a great event is when the newer generation of gaming machines come about. It is a thing that only occurs about once every five years. In the meantime we are totally left to guess what they will look like. People try and try coming up with images, going off of rumors, then, the moment that they arrive the look surprises everyone. There is a lot to wait for really. The new digital music release of a favorite artist, the next video game, next movie, next book, from our favorite people.

Great things have become a common commodity. Things like large TVs, computers, smart phones, the printer/copier/scanner, with a greater enabling of creativity from every person, the opportunity to express oneself more fully, to start small businesses in one's room, printing labels, gathering help, and so much more.

People are making their own T Shirts or whatever product they want to. When great sites like Amazon started they were still letting you use paper checks and paper money orders. You would go into the gas station or some place and tell them you want a money order for a certain amount. That was a paper you then mailed out to Amazon. You waited over a week for Amazon to respond and ship you your things. Credit card gift cards made it where anyone could more instantly pay for their stuff. Things have gotten better since then. We now have tracking available for certain services, seeing exactly where the delivery person is.

If you want a green marble, a twelve sided dice, cards, a particular shirt, stickers, stencils, a 90s trapper keeper, pogs, a sealed NES game, old Atari System, a clone of one, a mechanical video game, whatever it is, you can find it.

My Best Therapeutic Advice

If things are mostly well with you, then it is advice you probably do not need. You don't need anyone's advice if you are doing well enough. If you are having problems, then these may help:

They say to save your strength for when a problem does arise instead of drowning in fear before it comes (if it does.) In other words, deal with things as they come. You might be surprised at how well you can handle it. Who knows, things might be bad but not as bad as you assumed. For the sake of less stress, for the sake of happiness and fully enjoying life, do not fear, worry, or stress out about a possible bad future thing.

Do a good deed. Send a gift to a family member or loved one. Help out in some way, even secretly. A good deed could also be for yourself. It could be cleaning your place, taking a shower, getting rest. Do one good thing for yourself.

Gratitude therapy or what they used to call "counting your blessings" is when you take time to value your things. It can be a meditative sort of thing. To think of your things one by one and also think of all the good things in your life, bringing weight and value to them.

Keep busy. Even a little cleaning can feel good and lead to more, making you feel even better. Sometimes we have to force ourselves back into old hobbies. The start of a thing or a restart can require you to push yourself a little, but it is worth it.

Create a routine. Establish something to do at a certain time. From there, add things. Put together the kind of routine that most naturally fits you. Make one that you can depend on.

Use logic. Look for answers. Sometimes the solution to your problems are found by looking for answers, which sometimes are just little but helpful clues. You might have thought something was going wrong only to discover that it was not. It is a thing like "if this was true, then ( ), so it must not be true."

Gain pride, be bright sided. "Pace" all day long going over things that make you proud, optimistic, hopeful, and happy. During that time, think of any positive thing you can. Put life into a better perspective. Build around you such a strong wall that any bad thought is rendered powerless over you.

Choose to be strong. It is all too easy to slip into a state of self pity. Once we start regarding ourselves as a victim we become deeply hurt by it. Instead, be stronger than your problems and you will overcome them.

Shut others out if you have to. Give yourself some time to recuperate. Take a walk to distract yourself. Turn to focus on something worth focusing on over something that makes you angry and bitter. After all, it is your choice to find an enjoyable thing or to bear the negative feelings that arise from another.

And maybe life is better than you think it is at the moment. With so many opportunities for you to learn and grow, become stronger, better, to improve, to grow into maturity, and not go down the path of ruin as so many others do. You can say for yourself that you survived, that you became a better person, not someone who threw their lives away. And that is every good reason to be proud!

My Personal Hopes and Prayers

Here is my intimate wishes:

I pray to never be confined again. I have become greatly law-abiding. Wouldn't even jaywalk. Yet I fear jail.

I pray to be a part of God's Kingdom. The one on Earth? I hope that the Kingdom of Jesus is one like Earth right now only without suffering or mortality. A place like Earth I hope, with all of these technological advances there. Where I could have more to enjoy all the time but things are kept together by God. A place without violence for example.

I don't want to become the Antichrist. Given a choice I would not be so. With someone like me power can corrupt absolutely. I don't want the hellfire of being the Antichrist. I don't desire power or controlling people. I want something that I consider greater. To be in charge of "The Christian Satanic" people. That is my religious offering to God. It is the denomination I created. I would like to be like a gray shepherd to the gray people in God's Kingdom.

I pray to always have my family. That they don't die. That I don't die. That we are protected by God. That I always have them around. I hope that Jesus returns in our lifetime before any of them die. I pray that we are given immortality. I pray to not suffer through the tribulation. I pray that I do not worship The Beast. I pray to be raptured. I pray for Salvation and for the forgiveness of my sins.

I pray to always have a home. To not lose my things. That I have my place to live without being homeless again. I pray to continue receiving my medication. I pray for a safe and permanent cure for Schizophrenia.

I pray to not get sick. To not suffer. To not be harmed. I pray for God's protection. I pray for my health and to do well in life.

I pray for the scientific and technological advances needed to help the suffering. I pray for science and tech to help us with problems such as these: homelessness, hunger, starvation, crime, mortality, illness, being harmed, and I pray that universal basic income comes about.

I pray to be famous. I pray that I am talked about all over online. I pray for the success of my books and what they would do and bring about. I pray for the success of Christian Satanism. I pray for a better, brighter, and more significant life.

Please do not allow anyone to come into my life and ruin it. Do not let bad people have control over me. Let no lies be spoken of me. Let me be known for who I truly am.

It is my hope that death is something that cannot grind and chew up my life. It is my hope that divinities do not spit me out without me being heard and understood. That for the sake of the child I was, ever committed to the Bible, that I am saved once and forever. I was baptized when I was 7. I lived a rocky life but in the end became a good person. Someone who sometimes feels guilty about his past. Someone that only wishes well on others. And someone who has never lost his faith in God or His Son.

While the world falls apart I hope that I am seen through, guided and protected. That no evil harm comes upon me. With faith in God that things will be better someday. That I will be in His Kingdom not as a person seeking greatness there but a person who humbly follows His Will. I am a person that does not have ill intentions against others. I am human however, and yet require forgiveness in order to continue on into that new existence, where past inner hurt is no more. Where I can be my best person, but only if given the chance.

I have paid for the bulk of my sins. Being homeless, without money, in madness, with loss, confined, a wanderer, rejected, but have come into a life that I appreciate and fear to lose. I have matured in my life into a person who is no longer hateful.

These are my wishes and prayers and may they be heard by God. May God be with me always even after those times when I do everything I can to reject Him. May my mouth refrain from saying negative things against Him. May I not destroy Bibles or go off into an angerous bout. I will try to do well in life so that I will be seen as doing good upon the time of Christ's return and hopefully forgiven of all of my sins when that time comes.

Amen.

If Your Journey Starts Today

I once had been forced to choose to live elsewhere outside the cold winter of the poor city known as Albuquerque. "Where was I to do better," I didn't have any desire to live elsewhere for its sake alone. If it was to work at all with me there then I would have made it. My journey would be without money. My money was taken from me during the year I was homeless and lost.. Demented. I had much rather moved to NYC except that it was probably even colder there. Brooklyn would have been so nice. God put me on a pilgrimage and perhaps Satan had a part in that as well.

I had tested the waters. I had, at three in the morning, decided to leave my perfectly acceptable home as I was just looking for something better in life. My father grieved my departure, and I was gone for two weeks. That was the thing that later had homelessness thrusted upon me. Something like Shiva's trident piercing me. I have done things I am fearful to remember. Things that should have ended my life, while homeless in San Francisco. But I was seen through.

Maybe "all's well that ends well." My life has never been better. San Francisco is a nice place to live. My pure sibling (my only one, as opposed to my others being step siblings or half siblings) found her way in California as well. Maybe a gypsy kind of trait is found in us. If you ask for remarkable things then you can expect to pay a remarkable price. My wandering didn't start in San Francisco or even Albuquerque. I had been wandering for some time before that in a kind of off and on state. Living in shacks, barely having a home, not having what so many take for granted. Every kind of Church you could think of I attended and listened to. Every warning from a friend that I was losing it, I ignored. Once in San Francisco I decided to leave, to walk to an area I thought was San Jose (given my state it made sense.) I walked for days. I heard the voice in my head "this man is like a Beast, he's been walking for days." Then I came into what I thought was a new city. Walking a bit further I noticed that the sidewalk was made of red brick. I always followed the red brick sidewalk of Market Street. Then I looked up at the sign and it said "Market Street." I had been walking in a complete circle for days. Later that night a demon came unto me. He struck me with a metal pipe and told me to never try to leave San Francisco again.

Some are destined for a pilgrimage. It is their purpose. That is a purpose you are born into. Denying or fighting it will only make it worse and believe me, I struggled against it to the last. Do you belong to the sea? Do you belong to the edge of the world? Is there thunder inside of you? Once you are on the path to find the rabbit you may not cease until you are in hell itself. If Hell calls.. Your purpose can be anything too. From something small to something world changing. For good, sometimes for evil, and in my case the creation and development of Christian Satanism. The Holy has sparked those whom others are to serve, and sometimes hell does, too.

In the meantime things are being put together to make it happen. Not until remarkable things are achieved will it stop. Angels are powerful enough to set things up in your life that changes it, that guides you where the divinities desire you to be. That or the same with unholy spirits and the cause of a more profane force. Believe me, it was set forth before you were even born. Not until you can soundly reflect on your past will you know what was intended for you all along. If you are such a person then embrace it, do not reject it, because while it may be difficult and even painful, it is worth it.

Some Playlists

There is a different way of listening to music found here. I have two playlists for you, just for fun, one for God and one for Satan:

My Music And Videos For God

Billy Idol: Eyes Without A Face
No Doubt: It's My Life
A.O.S. History Repeats Itself
Garbage: Only Happy When It Rains
The Bangles: Eternal Flame
Jethro Tull: Bungle in the Jungle
Metro-Goldwyn-Mayer logo, "Tom and Jerry" Variant
Katy Perry: Roar
Legend: Loved By The Sun
Tori Amos: Crucify
Elton John: Yellow Brick Road
Meg Myers: Running Up That Hill
Wilson Phillips: Hold On
Nirvana: Heart Shaped Box
Devo: Whip It
Peter Gabriel: Sledgehammer
Alan Jackson: Just as I am
Fiona Apple: Sleep To Dream
Peter Gabriel: Solsbury Hill
Loreena McKennitt: Skellig
Goo Goo Dolls: Name
Michael W. Smith: Place in This World
George Harrison: My Sweet Lord
Ace of Base: The Sign
Frank Sinatra: My Way
The Byrds: Turn Turn Turn!
Michael W. Smith: Awesome God
Donna Lewis: I Love You Always Forever
Loreena McKinnit: Dante's Prayer
Cyndi Lauper: Time After Time
Joan Osborne: One of Us
Pat Benatar: Hell is for Children
Led Zeppelin: Stairway to Heaven
Gwen Stefani: Cool

My Music And Videos For Satan

LEXX soundtrack: Yo-A-Yo
Final Fantasy 7: Sephiroth's Super Nova
Malcom Mclaren: About Her
The Police: Wrapped Around Your Finger
Madonna: Ray of Light
Rihanna: Diamonds
Smashing Pumpkins: Zero
Journey: Who's Crying Now
Sound Garden: Black Hole Sun
The Cranberries: Dreams
Enya: Orinoco Flow
American Pop: Dishwasher Scene

The Gray Side

When the gray side begins the rest ends. Things are beginning to reach their own natural conclusion when it begins to appear and The Gray is the last of things. The Holy side takes on a great power and influence over things for quite some time: eras, ages. Before that there was nothing really. That is just a period of things coming into being. It cannot be called good or evil really. The Holy had yet to show itself. As for the iniquitous, when it appears it acts very quickly. That is because it is more according to nature. People crave the adultsy, the profane, even the grotesque, so it is no problem for music to move along on those terms. The same goes for movies, books, and everything else. In reality even Van Halen is Satanic, but look at how far the iniquitous has come! It pervades everything. Socially so, culturally, morally– it has brought about a new morality rejecting the previous Christian one.

Then after that there is a period of bringing it all together. In many ways people start to remember the past very fondly. Wanting a return to the past, in part, at least, or at least only halfway able to return to it. They have bartered to what should be kept and what should be lost. It is in the forming of The Gray that this happens. It is a tough choice: is this a hero or a villain? In the past there was no tough determination of that. But in the forming of The Gray such tough questions have to be answered. People want them answered, too.

It is when guidelines stop being followed that people take things in as they really should be. There are no longer any rules: this doesn't have to be designed on the Holy or Iniquitous. People have lost sense of what those even are. The wicked ways have become watered down so much that they've become strangely normal. People then go whichever way they will without any real sense of rules. Nothing is off the table. Things are no longer "side based." Anything can be done, and the beauty of both is taken in. Some people might lend more to one side than the other but only when that is a natural choice. The presence of both together is in fact itself a gray thing. It is just a mix like this: one person is doing the white thing, another the black thing, but still, that makes it gray. Gray can just be when both are present. Anyone at all taking in the whole picture becomes a part of it. It is the melting pot of both. It doesn't matter if one person is putting in the "good" and the other the "bad," it still makes a stew.

Inasmuch as it is natural to like and appreciate both the good and the bad it is natural to be gray. Gray is the natural magic, the true making of human beings, when it is that they are not constricted to be one or the other, not culturally, not by law, or whatever else.

We live in a universe of "two." "Two" is the nature of this universe. It is its design. It is easy to clearly make that point. Do you ever see a one horned beast or a three horned beast? I suppose they may exist but if they do they are rare. All of these ideas came to me while reading a book by Leonard Bernstein. He wrote that nature works in twos. He went over many examples. Even the clock goes "tick tock" to our ears. In reality the clock is going tick-tick but we hear it as tick-tock. Our heart beats in and out. Our lungs fill and remove. Our steps are one then two. We have two legs. Our lips are two. Our ears are two. Our nostrils are two, and it's the same all over our body. Two of us together make a new life. We have a night. We have a day. And most remarkably: our moon appears the same size as the sun. There is some mathematical magic to that. It takes the moon being at just the right distance compared to the sun. Which brings me to the next thing: it is the gray born of humanity. It is the ultimate thing that humanity creates. It comes about when both begin to dance together. It comes about when both meet and embrace. It comes because one or the other was never enough. It comes because things must continue to evolve and progress.

Wanting to be gray sided? First you must undo the shackles of being sided-minded. You have a great thing ahead of you if you do. Consider yourself a Gray Jedi in the making. (I don't think Jedi belongs in that term though no more than saying a "Gray Sith" does.) A "Jedith?" A "Sithedi?" You could be a gray magician. Just like all other gray things it is a brand new frontier and books or whatever else about it are hard to come by. That means less competition for you. Practice balance and moderation. Those show the power and value of gray sided practices. Almost any bad thing is not bad if moderation and balance are put to use. Maybe someday gray sided things will be all around us, in movies, music, books, TV, comics, games, shows, and everything else. Right now though we have the honor of being the first of our kind.

Just remember that being gray can also be going back and forth from one to another. After all it is those things that make us a whole. While there is not a lot of gray material to go off of there is always me. I have written extensively on the subject in order to give it the greatest start possible.

Videos From Lucifer Jeremy White

Mantrid Vs. Brizon
Interview With The Vampire: Lestat's Piano Sonata
Legend: Lily's Dark Dance
The Devil's Rejects: Free Bird
Gay Rainbow: Robot Chicken
Scary Movie: Wanna Play Psycho Killer?
Sausage Party: Honey Mustard Reveals What The Great Beyond Really Is
Ninja Gaiden 2 - The Dark Sword of Chaos: Opening
Teenage Mutant Ninja Turtles (1990) Opening Scene
Final Fantasy 8: Gatling Gun Attack (Against a Crab Robot)
Final Fantasy 10: The Spring Scene / Suteki Da Ne
No Doubt: Spiderwebs
Eric Idle: Always Look On The Bright Side Of Life (From Monty Python)
Samael: Slavocracy
Betty Boop: Judge For A Day
Blade Runner: Tears In Rain
Joker: Anarchy In Gotham (Ending)
South Park: Van Halen (World Unites)
Enigma: The Child In Us
Final Fantasy 8: The Ending
Castlevania Requiem: Fairy Song
Terminator 2: Truck Chase Scene
Final Fantasy 9: Melodies of Life
Poppy: Fill The Crown

Taking On Different Personas: Animals

Most people are pretty much just themselves while there are so many different types of people out there. Here is a lesson in broadening yourself by making you into so many different things, things you would have never known or experienced otherwise.

The Bird– Can just fly away from a problem, from danger. A bird is hard to reach. Is secretive in its coming and going. Is a discrete creature. A bird will never settle. It has a good view of the world overall. It looks down on humanity from great places.

The Bear– The bear is big. Is formidable. With one look at it, you know not to bother it. Yet it can be jolly, just as people hope it is. If you give to the bear then perhaps it will leave you alone.

The Bull– "Play with the bull and you'll get the horns." The only thing that works against a bully is to bully the bully. When moments of strength are called for, be the bull.

The Rabbit– The rabbit knows the ins and the outs of things. It is able to find things that others will never even know about. It has a trick up its sleeve. It is hard to pinpoint and locate.

The Goat– The goat knows how to get away from people and be with its own kind: in the mountains. The Goat is always looking for higher places. Like the higher class in their lofty places.

The Cat– The cat is a creature of fun. Of liveliness, one full of spirit, a fun getter.

The Mouse– The mouse cannot be captured so easily. The moment you think you have it is gone, is elsewhere. It goes quickly back and forth from places unseen, usually alone, and before you know it it is gone.

The Fox– The fox wins by appearance. It is to create a good image of yourself. To wear the clothes that those esteemed wear, no matter what those may be. Could be a uniform, a suit, an elegant dress. It is a high stature thing.

The Horse– The horse is steadfast and strong, determined, and steady. It is a thing of being solid and sure.

The Tiger– The tiger cannot be beaten and wherever it goes others know its place. It is a thing of authority, of ruling position.

The Elephant– The elephant is too strong to be stopped. It is backed up by powerful forces surrounding it. It doesn't worry where it goes. It has carefully prepared for all things and is harmless, yet unable to be harmed.

The Dog– The dog appears a bit dumb but isn't really. Its relationships matter. It is a friend to all. It is not without defending itself, however, if it must. The dog can be foolhardy but has its own kind around it to protect itself.

Taking On Different Personas: Types

The Soldier– The soldier picks his or her cause and fights for it. They have determined something to be a problem and know in their hearts that it is a thing they should fight against. It is the battlefield of a cause of their choice, whatever that may be.

The Fighter– The fighter will not let an injustice be ignored. They know when things are wrong enough to be dealt with, and do so. Whether it is a minor problem or a major one, they seek to fix it. Sometimes it is not about them but is about others who are suffering under an over-rule of bad people.

The Bard– The bard has chosen to make music the biggest part of their life. They know it is in a field of so many giants before them, even those of recent times. But they will put all they can into their art to be among the best of their kind. They can at least entertain in a small club or among their friends. They are entertainers at heart. People are known to appreciate such people more than any other kind.

The Prince/ess– To reach the higher stature of humanity whether it is in the framework of capitalism or more literal rule over people, a prince must be worthy. Only the best will ever find themselves in the truly higher class. Some have gotten there by inventing something, starting a major business, or through difficult schooling, unless they were lucky or were born into it.

The Magician– The magician works his/her magic from the shadows, unseen, changing the world itself as determined by the power they hold inside. The greatest of magicians have changed the world entirely. It all comes in many colors: some are cute Wiccan people that carry crystals in their pocket and pray to candles. Others are ritualistic. Some are more involved than others.

The Master– They take on the job of mayors, of governors, of any authority figure, if even just a security guard. That or something else: that they are just a person best at what they do. Among the higher, the most valued, in any profession. That includes the best musician out there, or artist, author, game maker, director, and so on. Among the greatest of masters in their profession are Beethoven, Mozart, The Beatles, Mark Twain, Stepen King, John Williams, Steven Spilburg, Tom Hanks, Tom Cruise..

The Pawn– The Pawn is a lesson in what *not* to be. It is a push over. It is a person whose problems overrun them because they will not do anything about it. It is a person who has little to no fight for themselves. That person that is just taken from again and again. A person easily fooled. A person that others take advantage of.

Spells and Equipment You Can Use (More Metaphors)

Fire– This is when you have a presence around you that goes outward, one of power. They that achieve greatness and notoriety are those that have "set the world ablaze." There is no stopping them from propelling into greatness. *Or something you could call Fire 2:* To bring warmth and the nurtured into your life. To have the protection you need, the sustenance you need, can be called *Fire 2.* Then there is *Fire 3:* Call it the burning away of past things in order to create a better future.

Ice– The preservation of better things. An ice spell lets you keep what you would keep. It works well with anything you need the most and feel that you must always have around. *Ice 2* helps either you or another (or a group of people) calm down. It has them cool off, so to speak. *Ice 3* is in preparation to make things better. It is the improvement that means the difference between something good and something with no value to you.

Water– Water is a spell of having something rush forth that you wish to go forth. *Water 2* is in having something people will always need, and being that person who provides it, to your benefit. *Water 3* is a washing and cleansing spell. That is in improving anything that needs to be improved, or changing anything you need to change, or to just make yourself a better person with a new start.

Air– The spell of air is to speak a prayer. To throw your voice into the universe itself. To have something entered into a new realm. A place you know exists. You can't so clearly see it, if at all, but you know that it is there and you hope it will talk back to you someday. It is like posting thing after thing online hoping for it to be heard. In whatever way it is like getting your voice around.

Lightning– Lightning is a rather strong statement or product of yours. Something that simply cannot be ignored. That once it appears it is seen by all. It is in any way being a strong presence. *Lighting 2* is to come in strong and fast. Like a lightning rush: so fast that it wasn't even seen. It is quick and powerful at the same time. *Lightning 3* is to energize any given thing until it is given life and able to roam about on its own. For some only a spark (a miniature lightning) is needed. For other things it may require a lot more power.

Reflect– "I am rubber, you're glue, everything that you say bounces off of me and sticks to you."

Quake– It is to rock the world with something great. To "shake things up." To cause a rumble and ruckus if you want. It is the power of a great new thing. It shakes the foundation of things before it. It does so so well that things must be rebuilt to stand it.

The Equipment, or, "Tools Of Life"

Sword– You should not only bear a sword but know how to use it when the time comes. You must be ready to pierce your foe when that foe comes too close. You must then be ready with an answer, a response, one powerful, that will defend you and keep others at bay.

Bow And Arrow– You must be able to identify your problem from far away and deliver it in an exact strike. Sometimes it is best to keep your target at a distance. A bow and arrow will give you the ability to undo it without getting too close.

Flute– Sometimes we need a peaceful repose. Sometimes we need only relaxation and calmness with nothing else that matters so much. It could be a good song of your own to carry you through. It is a tool that helps us drift away.

Gloves– Without the right power in our hands we may never come to know greater things. It takes strength to grasp and hold those things. A glove is like a diploma, the talented hands at a keyboard, or a hammer in hand forging a sword.

Shield– We must always be wary of dangerous people and never be "in the wrong place at the wrong time." A shield can be a security camera, well locked doors, not going out at night, keeping an eye on everything, or anything at all that could save your life. It is also in keeping bad things out of your life to begin with.

Treasure– The meaning for any journey is to gain the greatest treasure you can. So what goals do you have that would lead you to such things? What is it in life that you want the most? And how will you get it?

The Crown– Be a King/Queen of your own place. Find a good home, the best that you can. Your house is your kingdom. Hopefully none can ever take it from you even if it is rented. So have a good and comfortable chair (throne) where it is that you are in control and can freely decide what to do within it.

Call it "Lucifer's RPG." Create a Book of Shadows surrounding it. Write down which spells and equipment serve you best in life. Work on the personas until you have mastered them just right.

More On Magic

Stepping aside from the metaphorical form of magic/ RPG stuff I will return to the world of real magic.

RPG video games are a strong effort in making magic as real as it can be. When things enter into more and more realistic forms it can very well take an ordinary world and implant magic into it. I have always called such a thing "the second reality" when it is that the virtual world feels and seems just like a second reality. No wonder why Christians detest things like D&D so much. They could have at least argued that "magic isn't real" before that. I have an idea of a D&D type of encyclopedia. The letter C would contain Characters, contains Class, P would contain Places, S contains Spells, contains Shops, M would have Maps, and so on. Maybe the books would even have card sleeves in them. I have gone over all of it before.

I had a hard time finding black candles and even bells when I was young trying to perform rituals. Only at Halloween could you find any black candles and the only bell I had had a Santa Claus on it! That's no longer a problem however. In fact, neat little pentagram necklaces are cheap. This Satanic Panic stuff: I enjoyed it! I enjoyed being feared, being called The Devil at times, being the one in school that people should have nothing to do with. I was quite alone in Satanism however. I lived in a small Bible Belt town. Thanks to the internet a person can find all sorts of groups to be a part of. I however have lost interest in groups, but that is just me.

Numerology: for me, having considered different things and coming to my own conclusions: 0= pre existence, 1= an origin, 2= Life, 3= New life, 4= Stability, or groups, 5= Grace (it is a number I use to give myself a break such as being five minutes ahead or behind), 6= The Satanic Force, 7= The Holy Force, 8= Those going back and forth, 9= The Greater Conclusion, and 10= A return.

The number 8 is great. It is the black cue ball. It is the magic 8 ball. You should have 8 glasses of water a day. You should have 8 hours of sleep at night. The musical octave is an 8. There are 8 planets (some say) in our solar system. And oddly, Pluto is not really a Disney character either. The one that doesn't talk, anyway.

Tarot Cards: Tarot cards are a lot of fun. There are so many different decks available, and why have just one kind? They work by opening up your third eye. They give you an interpretation of reality that you cannot otherwise have. They bring things to your mind, sorts of ideas, sorts of abstract conceptualizations that you would not otherwise have.

Astral Travel: Mostly works during dreaming. I'll give you an example: I used to practice astral travel every night and at the time thought I didn't get any results. Then I realized that it was happening in my dreams. I was climbing higher and higher towards Heaven the nights after I fell asleep to astral traveling.

The Magical Alphabet and Language: There are some that are already available. It is more fun to make your own however. Lots of us do that. It is surprisingly easy and quick to learn how to write using supplemented symbols. Such as the letter A being a lightning bolt instead. In fact you could learn to write with your new symbols after writing with it for just a few days. As for supplementing sounds instead, one thing that I did was to find the sounds that different languages used for Satan's names (the highest devil from culture to culture.) and used those for sounds in my new magical language. Personally I think the most diabolical of sounds is *Ler*. The worst things have that ending sound.

I had quite a wicked idea of turning the Bible into a magic language. It sure takes a lot of computational power, however, the last I checked. It uses the find-replace tool on a word processor. You take one sound, then, and give it another sound. Such as replacing the sound of the letter A with something else. Or to take whatever sounds together and turn those into the sound of your magical language.

If you want to write your first book then a prayer book is an easy and beneficial start. Being as greedy or non greedy as you want. Sometimes being selfish, but not always. For a better world and a better personal life, a prayer book is a good idea. They are very easy to write, too.

Having twelve names as your inspiration. What are your twelve biggest influences? What have they done that you desire to do? In what way can magic have you achieve such a thing?

A lot of the time magic is about being friends with deities. If a crystal in your pocket is going to do anything it is because a deity that likes you thinks you are cute. You could write down your prayers to them and expect them to read it, if you do have spirits that are close to you. Be committed to them and avoid ignoring them, especially if you have some indication that they are in your life.

Ask for and seek the most powerful of things. Be exact in what you want. Be different towards that. "Work outside of the box." Ask for *a psychic connection to the world*. Seek to communicate with spirits, look for The Devil himself. Continue working on what you are working on and you may achieve great things.

Finding and Working On Your Purpose

There are perks and cool things about anything you choose to do. If it is what you chose to do you might like it for reasons not fully known by you. There is no telling really all of the reasons you like to do something but if you enjoy it they are there and take it for that. They might have for you just the right challenge, ease, a "wow" factor, and something that makes you proud even if you don't really know why. Such a thing was true for me. I never considered that writing can be done anywhere and that is something that makes it a cool thing, not until I heard another author bring it up. Whether it is on a smartphone, a tablet or laptop, or even on a paper notebook, yes, writing can be done anywhere. It doesn't make any noise either beyond some quiet clicking. It is a highly personal hobby too unless you have some weird person looking over your shoulder. What I also like about writing is that it relays so much more than anything else: be it a song, a painting, a movie, or whatever else. Besides, there is sheet music, books of art, and movie scripts that books can contain. So I have my reasons as to why I write. If you are to fully appreciate what it is you are doing, then having good reasons help.

We can do things we have never been able to do before, at least not with any practicality. Now we have a broad number of choices as to what we will do. An at home business can just mean getting a scale, packaging, and what it is you would sell. To have a thermal printer to print out labels, and simply mail it out. In making video games knowing how to program isn't necessary. There are things like The Game Maker software. Some choose to just do highly elaborate mods or hacks of old games. With music there is notation software. In fact some movies have music from such a thing and nobody would even know the difference. CDs or physical form albums are no longer necessary, or even ever used anymore. For our game we can have manuals produced in a large amount at a fair price. Because of 3D printing you can make action figures, toys, or a number of useful things. We can have our video games graded to get more money off of them. Some choose the lifestyle of rummaging through thrift stores to buy things cheap and resell them. They either have a spot rented out in an outlet, their own business, on or offline, or both.

If we want to have shirts printed out we can do that. If we want to make and sell stickers we can do that. Some have nice side money from doing so, in fact. What little shipping costs are involved in that are a nice factor as well. As with books: we can have those printed out and sold online. We could produce magazines that way if we wish to. Online companies just ask for a small amount of royalty– in all the cases I know of. People are brought forth and organized thanks to the internet. We know much more easily where the events are. In those events we can sell our best things or buy great things from one another.

Some other possibilities are: making jewelry, working on electronics (making small and simple devices if we want, or modding old game systems), turning scrap metal into bars such as of copper, or making things like display swords with it, being a star on YouTube if we are at all able to, wood working, working on our homes (something that is more possible than ever according to just the right parts we want), receiving instructions has become a great deal easier thanks to the internet, and perhaps creating a great new website.

Maybe your purpose is to be the leader of a group. One that you make just as well as you are able to and both serve and are served by. It could be a branch of something else or something new all together. One with its own religion based on the best influences of your life. Perhaps, unlike me, you are a spokesperson, more than you are just an author.

Time may only tell before you have chosen the thing you truly love to do. Hopefully over the years you will have come to master whatever it is you wish to do. To be a stand out person, one with a good income, doing what it is they want to do, as opposed to what another would have them do.

The Wide Array of Activities to Choose From

Apart from a purpose there are things you can do that are just pleasure based. I am very minimalistic. Maybe it is because I am getting older. I am mostly fine with TV and writing in fact. Although some iced tea and coffee is a good addition to whatever else it is I am doing. To me a good movie is good therapy. After our days of work are over and cannot really continue (though that doesn't happen to everyone) then we are left with some basic things or a life of vacationing, depending on who we are. For me it is just being in a small room being left alone, free to do his little things. I have in fact retired years ago, you could say.

Some are gamers at heart. I recommend emulators and roms if you cannot afford the new high tech stuff. Out of all activities, video games were the joy of my life. It really does appear to me that you either grow out of it or not. I think it is better to say "grow apart" though. I have no bad opinions of adult gamers. I in fact wish I still had the joy for them that I did as a kid and young adult. As a kid though, put me in front of a game and I will not leave until it is finished. As soon as I was home from school it went straight there. That was at a time when it was captivating to me. Those are days lost, unfortunately.

Some love to read. Some are happiest that way. They have the patience for it. They just enjoy the totality of going from one page to another until finished. I personally prefer Manga. I have been reading the Attack on Titan manga in fact. I have enjoyed a book or two. I really liked *A Dozen Black Roses,* some books by Anne Rice, *Hitchhiker's*

Guide to the Galaxy, The Magic of Recluse, and as a kid loved all sorts of books. I guess reading was still a novelty to me at the time.

Some enjoy spending their time listening to music. I think I am spoiled by the whole thing since the internet has given me any song I would ever hear.. Again, again, again, until it all lost its meaning for me. I used to be at a VCR on a music channel ready for the moment when my favorite music video would play, to capture it. Or the same with a cassette tape and the radio. When the internet came out I enjoyed all that past music that I hadn't heard in a long time. I envy those that enjoy music. I hate to say it, but I don't get anything out of it anymore.

I'll tell you what I do like. I like shopping. Some would even call it great therapy. I just don't like it when there are many people in the store. There is always someone looking at the same things as you are. I feel like I am in their way and they are in my way at the same time! But my greater joy comes when I am done buying and back at home with it all. I feel sort of accomplished by it. I now have those things I had been wanting. I have more than before and they are really nice things.

Some really enjoy time at the theater. I enjoyed that as a kid through and through. Now I am always just waiting for the thing to end. Not half of the movie plays before I am ready to leave, but can't, because my friend is my ride. That is usually the case. My mother used to bring a pillow and nap through the whole thing. As a kid I didn't understand why, but I do now. I have become more of a clip person. Give me a nice long clip and I will bring it all together over time.

Some love to collect things. The process itself is fun to them. That's one I can relate to. Flea markets are awesome places. You never know what they might be selling. Then you find that thing you have been looking for for so long and it is even at a nice price. Or to wander around online finding things to add to your collection. A convention perhaps, like one selling old video game things. To finally be the big kid on the block with the best games, where when you were a kid you might have gotten a few a year. People don't understand why they want to collect everything. Things they'd never even use in fact, but just want to have. In a case like that I would just say "why ask why?"

Some are into exercise. Some are even into tough bodybuilding. Others like to jog. Some like it in sports form. Then for some it is yoga, flexing, tai chi, or martial arts.

I have had a lot of fun watching people at their art. I have enjoyed videos of people working on electronics in a complicated way. They have all of these tools I know nothing about. They pop in and out parts effortlessly. They restore things long lost and dead. They have amusing small talk along the way. I have also seen people taking loads of junk metal and making bar after bar of pure metals from it. I have seen jewelry makers making their jewelry. I have listened to directors explain how their movies were made. I have heard great songs from freelance musicians. I have enjoyed listening to bands cover old video game music. I have found people online that ignore copyright stuff altogether and sold products of our nostalgia. I have seen a more ready and capable race of people producing what they do.

Being Successful/ Finding a Life of Greater Significance

First, be aware of the level of competition you are entering. Some things might be the easy thing to do but the easy things have greater competition to them. It might be easy then, yet a struggle. Always strive to be at least 50 percent better than everyone else. Most people are only willing to work so much. Work more than they do.

Be different. Be the only person of their own product. Be what is new and better at the same time. For that sake, make your influences obscure ones. Avoid being a copycat all you can. Avoid making the "ugly cousin." If you are an ugly cousin then people will say of you "not that guy again, who does he think he is?"

Keep in mind that some things are simply unpredictable. You might not know they would succeed until you try them. The first arcade machine that was placed in a store was thought to be broken at the end of the day. It only stopped working because it was stuffed with too many quarters.

Be with the times. Like in the early days of computers or video games, when those were a whole new field, and some entered into it at just the right time (early on) in just the right way. Some of those companies are behemoths in their fields to this day. It is better to enter into the game early than it is to enter into it late.

Be ready to change with the times. Don't keep selling film based cameras while everyone is getting digital cameras. Always be aware of those willing to do the same thing, only free, and look into the future to see if there is any possibility you will be outdone.

Get yourself out there. Don't assume that people will just find you. If you do then you can expect that the only ones who come to you have stumbled into you. The internet is like a thousand billboards, each of which are ignored. Be more of a person who finds others and brings them in, as much as possible.

Be the top brand. Focus on great quality. Be renowned for having the best of any given thing. Take time and care with what you produce and the higher price will reflect that.

Give people what they want and what they need. Fill in the empty spaces in life. Make a thing that brings things together better. Make yours the superior version– the one that works better. Have it be something that people can depend on and needs the most often.

Keep the faith. Remain determined. Consider the reward. Have pride in what you do. You may never know when your ship will come in but the only way it will is by your effort. At the end of the day you may fail but at least you tried.

The Greatest Comes From The Strictest

Whether it is through outer discipline or self discipline, being among the greatest requires it. The words "elite," "master," and "expert," cannot be thrown around. It takes lots of time, practice, and effort to rightfully call yourself among the best. That can come from a tough job, from education, a hand me down talent from your parents, or a long time on your own teaching yourself. There are some that make it look easy while if others were to try it they'd immediately fumble around. Things like intricate carvings, making beautiful things from something, and masterfully bringing it all together can take a lifetime to learn.

Perfectionism is their pride. Yes, nothing is perfect– perfect is a philosophy though. It means that you continue to evolve and get better until very little to no flaws remain in what you do. People over time will find the best way to do any given thing. The process of getting better requires practice. It requires knowledge along the way. It requires able hands and minds. Sometimes it requires avoiding dire mistakes. Even the best of them can crack up sometimes, but the best will continue anyway.

So a person enters into a university to learn all they possibly can. They learn from the lessons of the past. They learn from the past masters of any given thing. They then have a set of tools before them. Those tools are useful and can often be things they'd simply not have otherwise. Things that wouldn't have ever come to mind were they not taught them. On the first day on the job a person is undereducated on what to do. The longer they are around the more highly valuable they are as an employee. It could take years to find someone who knows as much as you, by then.

Knowledge is valuable. Mastery is valuable. It could position you to make the most highly sought out product out there. If anyone ventures into what few others do and stays committed to it then they can reach that point. After a certain amount of time something that was once difficult becomes second nature. So look for the right master in learning any given thing– those who have mastered it themselves, and enter into their apprenticeship. That could be by seeking them out, or finding them at a school, or it could be by teaching it to yourself.

Don't Underestimate Your Ability To Survive

The fears and worries about what bad may happen are often less than the actual experience. There are no guarantees in life. One bad thing can happen to the best of us that turns our world upside down, and it happens all the time. Always take into account that there are people worse off than you. If you had a rocky road but came into a better place than remember that too. I would accept every problem I have if I knew that my own life were to become as good as it is today. I would throw my hands up in the air and laugh at the problems I have today if I knew I'd go from vagrancy to this life. Yet the dumb little problems still bother me. There are people out there without a home. People that eat from the garbage and barely get by. There are people in other countries who live under a dictatorship. There are people with the worst of lots and taking it all in, kind of makes me feel selfish.

If we are stronger than our problems then there is a reduction to them right there. Like they say "when one door closes, another opens." I like to think that whatever it is that happened in the past led me to where I am today. I live in a nice place too. I live in a nice city, San Francisco, no longer in the poor state of New Mexico (with all due respect.) I have so many nice things and so on and so on. So I would say "all's well that ends well." For that sake it would be foolish to go back and change the way I did things. Sometimes it is just about "living to fight another day."

In fact it is those things that make us stronger. To give one more saying, "that which does not kill us will only make us stronger." We either whither or grow from difficulty. We either mature or become sociopathic. A bad day that didn't turn out so bad can bring a lot of faith. We cannot lose hope. Without hope we are ruined.

Making Your Case With The Higher Powers

They will test you. They will at first despise you. They have wrought a lot of pain during their own journey. Not before they were fully incorporated did they come into their own being. Being among them is being among the greatest anywhere. It is that place that few find. It is that place that most don't even bother bringing to mind. It is the people in those places who have achieved the greatest things. It is the most desired lives that they live. It is a life of riches, fame, and notoriety. It is in those places that Lucifer truly shines. It is where his very light is seen. It is full of super humans. It is occupied by fallen angels.

To step out in front of them by accident already proves your worth halfway. They know you were brought to them for a reason. You may have even been brought to The Devil himself. You will know if that was him or not. You will know by his dragon voice, his plump belly, and his harsh demeanor. You then may not know it, but your life is set on course to accomplish something great. Certain pieces will fall together to bring that about.

You must prove your dedication. You must always be seeking a life of greater significance. You must be willing to work. To continually work on that which you know in your heart you must do. "There's no rest for the wicked." Don't get me wrong, it may be just as likely that you have aligned with Holy Forces, among those that are called The Saints. A person of miracles as such, God's vessel. Just don't be fooled: you might be the vessel for a false religion. To the person it seems like an angel visited him or her, which was in fact a jinn, devil, or evil spirit. They create pawns sometimes. Other times they are more purely Satanic, from Satan directly.

Those that look for a greater life will find it. That is, as long as they keep looking. They refuse an ordinary, mundane, or mediocre life. For most, it is a life of mostly work with just a little rest. When our purpose is given it must be taken seriously. If it requires that your life be turned upside down to get things out of you, then that could happen. Whatever it takes to make you best at what you do, you can expect it to happen.

Be dressed for such an occasion and at your best. Be mindful of who and what you are. Bring to mind the kinds of things that help you figure out what was meant for you all along. Especially considering things that only you are likely to do while with others it is a thing that never crossed their mind. The truly Satanic Elite may chew and spit you out but they are always willing to hear what you have to say.

Damned Be The Person Who Takes Your Livelihood

I got to attest to mandatory cleaning.. As imposed by landlords, unnecessary, and done by some money grabbing company. That *is* a problem of mine. Having to be gone for eight hours…

When I lived in a group home I was always ripped apart from what I was doing and sent on some activity. So I went from what I liked to do to sitting in the park or some other lame thing. I am grateful for the home they gave me. Am grateful for what they taught me, too, like cleaning my own place (which is what I meant by "unnecessary.") I have a clean place and I don't need them in here for eight hours. Especially when I have no money at the moment. Having money I would go to a restaurant and go see a movie or something, even just rent a different hotel room for the day.

I understand that they have these kinds of things in a group home. They are a place of transition. What about me, though, a person who truly likes to be alone. They are quick to say and fully believe that everyone needs to socialize. If I could request one right it would be to be left alone. I feel like I always have these forks being stuck into me and people with eye monocles staring me down. If there was something wrong with me they'd know it. What they don't know is that it is them that is wrong with me.

People don't have anything better to do. They are paid to do these dumb little things. It is like they are bottom feeders. If they are feeding off of me then they are truly bottom feeders. I have been treated at the level of a child in my time. My time as an adult. I went from my parents to government parents. It is good in some ways. You don't have to work. You just have to focus on treatment, but you don't have to work. It is a life though where you are babied.

The last I saw my biological father he threw me out of the house knowing I would be homeless. That was a sort of pleasure for him. While I was living with him (on social security, buying food for everyone, and paying rent) I had to go to the mental hospital once. He must have said to everyone "let's throw away his things and kick him out of his room" because when I got back that happened. So I was homeless then and in the freezing cold, and moved two states away (to the edge of California) to San Francisco. I made my own life here. I did so with great difficulty. I overcame the very worst. Even in insanity I found life very enjoyable at times. It is *my* life. It is the life *I* made for myself. I can say that more than just about anyone else. People can't just come in and give me this requirement and another for how I will live, I will not have it.

My greatest weapon against it is the books I write. It is my great assurance and insurance. It cuts a path for a better life. It brings me the hope of fame. It gives me the opportunity to be someone, someone who is heard. To be someone that is listened to, which means that my voice is loud and says "get out of the way." For that sake I have written over fifty books in the last six years. With more to come, even this one, a book that will take me about 10 days in total to get out there. One after another, building my case, slowly but surely. Then even if I am ever homeless again I can at least know that I am found everywhere online.

Life In The Mental Health System

Keeping with treatment was difficult for me when I lived in the small town of Clovis, New Mexico. The pharmacies ran out of pills. They'd give you a half a bottle and have you return. The mental health clinic I went to was a greedy one. They have helped me through a lot, but would require frequent therapy and psychiatric visits. Transportation was the worst problem. They didn't have a regular bus. They had instead a van that you called in a day ahead of time. You gave them a time to pick you back up and were often an hour late. The appointment time itself took a long time to even get in. The waiting time was long. I thought this was how it was all over. Clovis had no such thing as a group home or boarding care or SROs, or Co-Ops, and so on.

I came to San Francisco homeless. When I am crazy and unmedicated I think things like 'the doctor is trying to lobotomize me.' Being homeless and schizophrenia goes hand in hand. Fortunately there is effective treatment for schizophrenia. Makes you as sane as can be. In the meantime you are just crazy and wandering around, crazy and full of delusions. I heard voices. I heard them even when no one was around. I thought people were saying things that they were not. That it was always about me. Things like insults, often. Making sexual remarks towards me. For me the radio did the same thing. I thought the people on the radio could see and hear me, and were always commenting about me.

I had SSI at the time I came to San Francisco. Unfortunately I had shopped at a Target in New Mexico which had a data breach. So my "payment card" known as a "direct express" card was canceled and a new one was sent to my last address in

Albuquerque. More than a thousand miles away. Calling for a new one to be sent to me did no good. I tried again and again with "general deliveries" which is a mail service for homeless people, but never received it. I think it was three or maybe four times that I tried, waiting two weeks each time. Nothing came. Maybe in my crazy mind I didn't even give the people on the phone the zip code.

California has made it where the homeless can be "forced" into mental health treatment. It was a controversial thing to set up. Those that oppose it must not know just what a great difference that medication can make for schizophrenic people. If this was true at the time that I was homeless then I would not have suffered what I suffered through. I might have even been spotted and helped very early on. After a while though you lose all sense that there is anything wrong with you. After all, people who know they are crazy aren't crazy.

I have been in mental hospitals. I have been in them at least a dozen times. The longest time out of them was for nearly two years while every other visit was only two weeks to a month. Getting back on medication is like waking from a dream. Things finally start to come together– rationality, sane thinking, with the delusions slowly going away. Then there comes a time when you realize that those thoughts you had before were not true. The radio becomes just the radio again. Nobody is talking about you. No one even knows you. They are just going to the store or something. You can freely walk down the streets sane where at one time you wandered them totally disconnected from reality.

I had to receive shots at times for refusing medication. That would be the worst experience of mine. I wouldn't say I was ever abused. I wasn't. It isn't like it seems in the movies and things where people are being lobotomized or put into straight jackets. In a jail an isolation room is this room you may never leave except to shower and use the restroom (or for me where I shat and drew with my feces all over the wall.) While in a mental hospital it is called "quiet time," with the door creaked open, and you aren't inside for very long. After I was in jail in isolation for a month they sent me to a mental hospital. I had paranoia against them. When they put me in a rubber room I feared that I was never going to be let out. I feared things like being operated on. I went from a strict and harsh setting to a gentle and understanding one. When I arrived at the mental hospital that time I was surprised with how much they trusted me. Those in the jail had me in a spit mask strapped down to a rolling chair. The food was better. The food was always good in those places. Most of the ones I was in, anyway. I remember at least one that had things like pig fat "meat" and some other things I just couldn't stomach.

They are all pretty much the same across the board. There are some differences to them however. One might have a gym and even a game console to play with. Basketballs, with music playing loudly in the gym. They might have a nice library of books. They might even have a computer and internet on it. That was so with me once, and I thought I was too much a threat to the world to have internet access or even be allowed a pen to write with. You normally start out unable to leave for the food serving area. So they bring the food to you in a fashion. Many of them let you smoke cigarettes at certain times, normally four times a day. You are just taken out into the yard to do so. Most of them have "groups" which is when you gather to learn things, usually based on therapy. Some of the groups may include listening to music, watching a movie, art work, or whatever else.

One place let me have a radio. I had to break off the antenna to my pocket radio before I could have it. It is like not being allowed shoe strings or belts. As for a "belt" they have this small thing that brings together two loops in your clothes. That instead of something long enough for a person to hang themself. I have slit my wrist twice. I have consumed poisons. One time I was sent there just from overwhelming grief after my grandfather died.

My longest stay was for nearly two years. It was in the criminal section of the mental hospital. Believe me, that is the worst place in the mental hospital to be. Many of the people there are there for the first time. I would hear them joking about being there. If they determine you are incompetent then there you go. It isn't a way out however. As soon as you are normalized they return you to jail and 9 times out of 10 you proceed with your trial. You have to be there for three years otherwise. The law says that anyone who pleads insanity and succeeds is given twice the amount of time in a mental hospital than would have been for the highest prison sentence. Most of my time there was just spent pacing around and listening to my radio. I was put on the strongest of antipsychotics, a pill that gives me panic attacks sometimes. One that requires monthly blood work. A pill that I have been on for six years.

I was put into a group home. I was doubting they even existed based on all I knew in New Mexico. The first group home I was in was the worst of them, by far. You have to get up very early and start the groups (normally a therapeutic lesson.) And that goes on until mid day. There were lots of chores. You had to have a roommate (as it is in every group home.) That drove me mad and I am surprised I never got into a fight over it. I was helplessly rude to my roommates however. The littlest sound set me off. I had to learn to not get into fights though. You can shoot your mouth off as much as you want to but if you get into a physical fight you will be kicked out.

Chores in a group home are simple enough.. Most of the chores anyway. Some are harder than others. Some are just sweeping while another is carrying out the garbage and sending the trash bens back and forth from the curb. It's fair though in that the chores cycle from week to week. Another common thing is that you help cook food. So you cut, you grind on a cheese grinder, gather and so on. Once a week you cook your own meal for everyone, entirely on your own. You also go to the store with staff to get all that you need for your meal.

There are lots of walks and outside activities for people in group homes. They might just go to a park, a movie maybe, maybe an art gallery, or any number of other places. It can require a lot of walking, too.

You can't have food in your room (mice) and you can't have any kind of over the counter medication, not even antacid pills. There is a large TV for everyone. Towards the end of it you are being transitioned into a new place. That was a process that pretty much starts the moment you arrive, however. It can take a while to get you into your next place so you start right away. Normally you are in these places for three months to half a year. There is an outside area to smoke. That's pretty much everything there is to a group home.

I was in a "boarding care" at one time. My fears about being in my own place (like my own hotel room) was that I would mess up on taking my medication. So I wanted a place where the staff makes sure I take it. So I moved into one of these places. They are places of high care needs. In retrospect that didn't suit me. They clean for everyone, cook and feed for everyone, doing things like cleaning your room and doing your laundry. Early in the morning there is food. Then twice more in the day as a normal three meal a day thing.

There are Co-Ops. That is where you share the same building and may or may not have your own room. The difference between that and a group home is that you can do whatever you want to in there without being made to do anything at all, really.

And the SRO where I am currently housed. That is, a hotel for the mentally ill. It is a bit different from ordinary hotels. There are staff downstairs. They might check up on you from time to time. We are all a part of the same kind of people here. It is a more socializing kind of building. There is a TV and kitchen and a shared bathroom. Other than that it is the same as any other hotel. Oh, and the price is adjusted as it is for low income people.

My life is about getting my medication and doing my bloodwork for it. Sometimes I have panic attacks which are horrible feelings. Other than that I am pretty mentally well off. I have stress and worry sometimes. Nothing that would ruin me, I guess. I guess my biggest fear is losing my home. In this life housing can be a fragile thing but fortunately I have a payee who is responsible for keeping me housed. I feel that I am in a place where I would like to stay as long as I can. I had been wandering around my whole life up until a couple of years ago when I moved in here. On the other hand, maybe I am too settled in and kind of controlled by it. At least out on the streets I didn't have any worries.

I am lucky to live in the country that I do. I am even luckier to be in San Francisco. I have a lot going for me here. A nice bus system. Timely appointments, a dependable pharmacy, more possible living arrangements, and an EBT card. At one time I was seriously starving. At one time I slept in a shack and would wake up to tics on me. I had body lice while homeless. I even tried to kill them off by spraying Raid all over my body. Then just the fact that I was wandering around insane for so long. I hope those things never happen to me again.

Going With The Flow And Going Against The Flow And Going With The Anti Flow

Blending in is always a good practice. Like they say "when in Rome do as the Romans." There is no need to have yourself stick out like a sore thumb. By nature, people and groups of people do not like that. It is a sure fire way of getting yourself hurt. People are going into immature rants and are quick to violence when it comes to modern causes. There are some avenues however where you can be different and express it. Within things that even desire such a thing. Still there are modern rules which if you don't adhere to could get you ostracized.

I call it "going with the anti flow" when a person does things so differently that it leads them to different places, different conclusions, and works towards different results. It is an art where you are guided by yourself instead of being guided by someone else. It means to *deliberately* have contrary opinions. Even if it is just in consideration unlike so many who believe that things should be "left off the table." Your private opinions can be your own, and you should have them. Don't give your enemies the privilege of even knowing them however, because they are looking for them and when they find them they will use them against you.

Things like information and knowledge can be used against you but the less a person knows about you the less they have that can be used against you. Be a quiet person without much to say. Even when you are told something rude, there is a power behind not saying anything, as though what they say doesn't matter.. Doesn't register. Wasn't heard.

The newly popular isn't the old popular. It is a step beyond that. It is the next thing. Depending on how good and attractive you are at making the new thing.. To modify whatever in just the right way, knowing what is better than before, is how you become popular. So many however would take the "modern popular" to no ends, not ending the style of it until the next thing comes about which everyone must fully embrace. A person ahead of their time finds the next best thing. A person behind the times does not budge until that thing is apparent. Some see into the future, some see into the past, and some only see the things of today.

For any rule where there are a thousand who follow it, the one that doesn't will be the most adored. Beethoven and Picaso broke many of them. Many great musicians "overstepped" their boundaries. Beside them were the fearful lot that felt they must adhere to traditional designs. Some will follow after the original rule breaker. If they were not the first however, then they are only taking the right that that rule breaker gave them. It is not so "rebellious" you could say.

Besides, what is good at all about just doing what everyone else does? By being an individualist you are a long way there already, towards producing things that are different. That means having a taste and opinion that is different.. It means having different inspirations. It also requires that you know a good thing, something that others are yet to know, and only you can teach them about it. Yet some things are tried and true and those things should be identified as such. Sometimes what works best will always work best. With those things people don't want what is different. They want what is familiar to them and is most naturally desired. In some cases the best thing to be found has already been found.

What It Means To Be A Good Person Or A Bad Person

It means that mistakes will be made and to expect them. People make mistakes against other people.. That is human. Some of us have had very bad influences. Some of us have been abused. Some of us have been driven into bad lifestyles and just live the only lives they know. Unfortunately a person can go from someone good to a monster. There are monsters around us. We would do well to stay away from them. Evil exists in the world. Certain places can be frot with danger. I believe that for the most part, however, that people are good. Everyone deserves at least a little respect unless they go around causing harm to others. Hopefully the person I am speaking to is a good person. Someone who you might even call a person who tries to do their best good in the world and towards others.

Jesus Christ had a lot of teachings about that. In a world of wickedness, selfishness, hedonism, dog-eat-dog kinds of things, his words continue to speak of a person that is just as good and as gentle as could be.. A lamb of God. I have found his teachings useful in so many ways. They are words that let me accept the wrong done in my life instead of ever fighting. I have reduced my personal anger a great deal. They are words I used to mature with. They are words that brought about a philanthropic mindset for me.

Life is a struggle from the beginning to the end. We will never be fully without worry, concerns, fears, problems, upsets, pain, suffering, while we are on this earth. Always keep in mind that this is true with everyone. When someone seems to be going around angry on any given day, maybe it is that they just had a bad day. Even before we must deal with our own final day on this earth we must deal with the loss of loved ones. I remember the days of celebrating Christmas as a child. Those days are no more. The people who mattered most in bringing it together for us have passed on.

The best life to live is not one where you are always fighting. The best faith to have is faith in the good. The good is something you can depend on more than you can depend on things like revenge or acting poorly against others in whatever way. Maybe when the time comes people will acknowledge that you have tried your best to do well.

Maybe they won't be angry at you in the meantime. Perhaps they will even give you a helping hand when they see you need it. Maybe that help will come from God Himself when it is that no other will.

Just one wrong push, just one wrong moment of spitting in someone's face can mean the difference between being free or being locked up. Some have pushed old people to the ground which for them was an eventual fatality, then the law was all over them for murder. They went home that day. They forgot what they did. But then, out of nowhere, they were arrested for murder! More than ever people think they have rights that they don't and any opposition to their over-and-harmful-liberality must be heroically struck down "for the people." So they mess things up the worst way, they rant and yell and cuss, then call the police as though they were total victims, thinking the police would arrive and declare that "you cannot abuse her rights!" and lock them away. Only that doesn't happen. To their astonishment she is locked up instead. It does not go any better for a person that harasses the police. They might have had just one small thing to deal with: a ticket or something, but took it as a grave and abusive injustice, leading to behavior where the police had no choice but to lock them away. Police are people too, and if you ridicule them they'd respond in a human way.

It is up to us to decide what makes us either good or bad. For some it is in clinging to traditional things.. Former values. For some that means to have a job and work hard at it. For some it means they must stop taking drugs. For others it means starting a new diet. For others it means joining and doing well in the military. For others it means raising the best kid they possibly can. For another it means a good education. For another it means creating a great thing they work hard on. For some it just means being an honest person. For others it means to get off the gambling habit or smoking habit or to cut down on drinking alcohol. The point to make is that we have our own ways of being good people, becoming better people, or not being a person with harmful vices.

Whatever it is, you deserve respect for trying. You deserve whatever good place you have brought yourself into. Only the worst of people would try and take that from you. The kind who have no understanding or regard for others, only they would try and take that from you. They are the "what makes you think you are special" sort of people. They cannot do what you have done. And "misery loves company."

Currently people are encouraged by one another to blatantly break the law. They have lost a sense of punishment for what they do. The more who are among them doing the same makes the choice of doing wrong easier. They look outside and see a riot, and decide to loot, "they can't catch us all." They are quick to throw punches and vandalize, just for the sake of doing it. Unfortunately most people do what most people do. Such things are a threat to decency, civility, and peacekeeping people have a difficult job ahead of them, if it is even possible in some instances. One thing we need are tougher laws. And we need God's wisdom more than ever before, and I am not talking about the *false* Christian teachings that are going around. That Holier-Than-Thou attitude will not do.

Finding Your Tastes Is Finding Yourself

Hopefully your tastes are not mundane or lacking in any way. Hopefully they are just as unique as you. The more we consider them the more doors open. The broader our tastes are, the more we like, and the more we like, the more we appreciate.

The best route is in thinking in "best of" terms. It is a thing that should be specific, too, instead of just being general. So we have the "best of candy," the "best of hard candy," the best of "chocolate bars," the best "suckers," and so on. With food, find your favorite sandwich, soup, pizza, pie, hot dog brand, bread, and so on. My favorite pizza is the pan style containing mushrooms, pineapple, green bell peppers, and black olives. My favorite bread is potato bread. What's yours? Then there are drinks. What is your favorite juice, soda, tea, herbal drink, chocolate drink, and do you like apple cider or eggnog? Personally I like cherry cider the most although it is difficult to come by. I also like guava soda, a kind from Mexico. It comes in a glass bottle and has a pink color to it. It's great. My brother likes apple juice. I think that happens to be one of my least favorite. I like grape juice myself. I also like rice water which is a thing. I am big on drinks over all.

Nostalgia is a good place to turn to in finding more to like– or to decide to continue to like, in remembering it. I really like a lot of things from 1988-1992. I don't know why exactly. Must have been a sweet spot at my age. I was 8 years old to 12 years old at the time. It is a rule with exceptions though. I like the neon colors of the time. Things were given that extra touch. Fanny packs, I still use them, whether or not they are popular they are useful. I like POGS, and I certainly like retro gaming things. Was into TMNT and into certain occult/ Satanic things, but into Christianity too, and would try my hand in other religions. Some are fortunate when it comes to nostalgia. They appreciate things just as much as they did when they were kids. I have such a sense but not a powerful one.

You might decide what makes up your clothes. I have gone with cargo pants, hooded sweaters, certain kinds of jackets, outdoor sandals when at home, and more expensive shoes for outside. I liked trench coats for a while but people didn't like them so I stopped wearing them. I used to wear long johns. They do keep you much warmer. We have had a warm winter in San Francisco though, and often do. I bought two rings which together are worth about $1,000. One of them from Nordstrom, a "Bony Levy Snakeskin Gold Ring." There are lots of ways your taste can go when it comes from jewelry. The color of sapphire that you prefer. If you like pearls, or black pearls. What do you think of turquoise, or jade, or do you just want something in gold or silver?

Some people like video games. Some like very engaging games such as an RPG. Others never got into RPG games. They in fact may like the opposite of "engaging" preferring the "leisurely." A leisurely game is one that you can pick up and beat within half an hour. You can continue longer if you wish, but that is your choice. Those are sports games, fishing games, racing games, card games, gambling games, puzzle games, and so on. I really like metroidvania games myself. I like turn based RPG games, which for a time were going away but have been present in some of the newer games again, at last. It is a nice and versatile hobby if you like games to begin with. There are a lot of choices. Some like strategy games, others fighting games, some like shooters, others like platformers. Some like new games. Some like old games. Some are fine with the cheaper stuff. Others are eager to get the next gen console.

Do you like to read? What kind of book do you like the most? A mystery, a romance novel, horror story, science fiction book, or books on vampires? Some prefer their reading to come in comic book or manga form. As a kid I liked to choose your own adventure stuff. Actually as a kid I would pick up just about any book and read it. One time I really enjoyed a book about mysterious monsters such as the Lockness Monster and giant squid. Others just read whatever is before them online. Of course I appreciate a reading person, such as you.

For some it is the choice of what pet they would have. A cat, a dog, a snake, a hamster. Some have a motorcycle lifestyle. Might even be in a club for such. There are a lot of choices between alcoholic beverages too. You can tell each of them apart and finding your favorite means trying all that you can until you come across what is best for you. That is, if you drink at all. I did just that and came up with a Blue Hawaiin. I don't drink at this time in my life. When I did I liked things like Rum and Budweiser Red. Some smoke tobacco. I am one of them. Am not either proud or not proud about it. It is just something I am stuck with. I would switch to vaping but it is no longer legal here, at least not in flavor or nicotine-containing form. That's fine though, you should put the children first.

Then there are the silly and often childish things we may like. One of my favorite of them is glow in the dark star stickers. You stick them on your ceiling and maybe you've heard of them. There are glow sticks too. EL panels are even better. They have a glow in the dark effect only they are electronic. Those are more commonly known as indiglo and are found on many watches. I remember the first time I saw someone with such a watch. It was in a dark bus and someone asked for the time. He pressed a button and the whole bust lit up a bright green. Before that we were using these tiny tiny little bulbs! Anyways– I would also list green marbles, little green army men, twelve sided dice, board game pieces, miniature figures, action figures, toy keyboards, mechanical games, pocket magnetic games, stencils, color pens, spirograph sets, trading cards, mood rings, POGS, tokens, toy flutes, various stones and crystals, stickers, Halloween pencils (has a bright orange eraser with things like black cats on them), Halloween pumpkin buckets, fiber optic lamps (impressive if you have never seen them), troll dolls, video game manuals, and Mickey Mouse watches. I like all of those things. There is much more to be found. Visiting the toy aisle is always worth it. Some adults do like childhood things. Unfortunately it doesn't go far beyond action figures and old video games for them.

So.. have you ever tried a Rueban sandwich? Some Baklava? Listened to some good 1960s music? It was twenty years before my time, but I found lots of good stuff in that period of music. Some of the best music has long been forgotten and some of it was never popular to begin with. We can find just the right shirt online. Whether it is an eye of providence shirt or taken from a scene in Zelda. We might come to like a kitty Cat clock or a lily lamp. We might find older types of things superior to the newer kind, which replaced it. We can then laugh at the people who settled on an inferior thing, having the old thing all to ourselves. We each have our own favorite soap, body wash, and deodorant. Some of us cannot stand a polyester blanket and must have a pure cotton blanket instead. Some have considered these things and others have not. For some, things are all pretty much the same. Those that do consider these things will broadly open the doors to better things.

Having a Stronger Will.. Being More Willing

I make it a habit to only nap once a day, if at all. It is a rule I do not break. Otherwise I could come into my past state of sleeping all the time. That is a depressing thing, as though you are just wanting to lay dead. I put things into my routine until I build one that I can depend on and have faith in. As a result I know what I am doing every day and what I will do the next. I don't have these empty blotches of nothingness in my life. Routines are good to have. Sometimes it takes a while to make them stick. Sometimes we just give up on a thing halfway through, but we must keep trying.

It takes a lot of bravery and personal power to do something you never do. To just decide in a moments time to go see a movie when that is just something you never do, to suddenly pick up a book and start reading it when that is something you never do, do suddenly go get a canvas and paint and just decide to make a painting, when that is something you never do, these things are among the most powerful things you can do. There is always exposure therapy as well. You may be bombasted with knowing the whole process is too much. In a case like that do not think about how much it would take, just do the first step, that's all. Ignore the rest. Buy one thing towards a new hobby. Like with cleaning: tell yourself you are just going to sweep the floor and that's it. You would be surprised with how quickly you think "I will wipe down the counters as well," and before you know it you are cleaning the whole house.

We all have hobbies that we once spent a lot of time on. We loved doing them. We thought we would always be doing them but somehow we stopped. That isn't always a bad thing. I would say you like what you like. If you had decided on something new that just stuck with you then that's fine. If you feel at all that you are cheating yourself though, then consider that first step kind of thing. Things like that can take a lot of will. It is a powerful form of will to have.

In the military they teach you to do things as they say them when they say them, without thinking. Regular people fiddle around and become confused when there is someone yelling at them to do something. People in the military become such that the confusion is gone. The feeling of urgency isn't so much there. They can then do things as they are told to them quickly and without problem.

Breaking away from our necessary tasks can cost a person a lot. It can cost them their home if they allow hoarding into it. They could come into living in a garbage filled mess. They could get maggots in the dishes they do not wash. They could be overrun with feces and roaches if they do not clean up after their pets. They could smell badly and not know it, they could build scraggly beards they never trim. They may wear the same clothes for days at a time. Becoming late for work becomes an everyday thing until they are fired. They might have fixes in their home necessary. They might own a property they never take care of and lose it to natural damages. They might over eat or under eat.

A weak will is something important to work on. It is a thing of great importance and can either make or break someone. A weak will allows the dictation that you will not get up out of bed in the morning. A weak will allows the dictation that you will not study that night on your college courses. It makes you abandon a job without really trying. It causes you to stop halfway or even at the point where you are nearly done. It makes you devour food without restraint. It makes us irritable and impatient. It devalues our self control.

A strong will is a good thing to have. It makes work a natural and frequent ability of ours. It leads us past knowing the piano a little to mastering it. It takes what may have been minimally done to what is mastered. With it we can be sure that what we start we can finish. Without it we fail at even trying. With a strong will we accept and understand defeat but keep on trying. We continue to look for answers and improvement until we find them. Without a strong will we take any excuse to quit. We will shower every day or at least often enough even if we do not like the shower. We will only become better at our jobs instead of going from one to another all of our lives. Yes, a strong will is a good thing to have.

Other Things That Are Good To Have

Hope is a good thing to have. Disaster never strikes so hard when we have it. Without it, we are ruined by it. That strike can tear us all apart. Can make us a bit mad. Can have us looking helplessly for answers that are not there. It takes away our patience. If our answer is not there when we want it we start to fear it will never come. We feel abandoned. We fear *someone else* is crushing our hope. We think things such as it was stolen, misplaced, intentionally never sent. A person of greater hope is more likely to think some mistake happened or there is a reason for it all. A person with hope knows that one way or another they will get something fixed. It is not a catastrophe. They have the power to sort things out.

When it is that a person's hopes are crushed though, that is just about the worst thing you can do to someone, especially to a child. I had a parent that promised to take me to the flea market to buy things on my birthday. A cruel trick was played on me though because I knew it wouldn't happen– to some extent. To another I felt I must have done something wrong, but didn't. There were promises again and again– will get you a dirt bike, so I poured over a catalog of nice parts for one. Without too many of my own examples I can say that doing harm to a person's hopes is a true crime. The price that parent paid was no longer being my father, instead turning that title over to my step father.

Patience is a very good thing to have. It fixes so many problems in life while making everything else better. A patient person does better at work and self care. They make better things instead of rushing through them. A work ethic is good to have too. Teaching your kids to do chores is an important thing, as is an allowance for it.

A good education is a great thing to have. We largely cannot have the great wealth that few others do. If we are not born into it or strike it rich with a lotto ticket then our best alternative is a good education and if it is based on a profession you really want to have, then all the better.

Maturity can make the difference between living where you want and being free from being locked up for ranting and raving at some poor business. It is surprising how much maturity is lost from the people of today. Doing well with others will take you far. Always being a disruption can cause all sorts of problems for you. Like Paul said: be all things to all people.

A talent will always give you something to do and become better at. It can be a source of pride and the opportunity to become a higher statured person. The better you get at it the better chances you have at making a difference. Besides, you will just have something to show off with.

A good home is one of the best things you can have. You will be spending so much time there. It will keep away the bad weather (unless the weather becomes atrocious.) Gives you a bed at night. Gives you room to collect every little thing you want. Gives you time alone, for some.

Determination is a good thing to have and in fact we will not always have to have it. After some time in doing any given thing as best as we can it turns into a natural habit. "The rest is the icing on the cake." We can accomplish great things and there aren't even many ways we could be doing any better. So just keep in mind: you will not always have to be finding determination. After some point or another it will become a kind of automatic thing for you.

     Self restraint, balance, and moderation are also good things to have. Not much is considered a vice when you restrict how much you do them. A person that buys a scratcher once a week might hit it big.. In a few years or a decade. It never wasted their money. Could practically be called an investment. A little alcohol can relax you. You might not even get a hangover. Letting our money go a little at a time brings more pleasure to buying and you never know what you may have forgotten to buy if you spend it all at once. Then a day won't come where you think you should have bought this or that. Cleaning as you go along is a good thing. You don't burn yourself out on it. As is with work in general. A slow and steady pace is better. Instead of having to do everything at once you are never too far away from having it be done. I think the smartest people do not make A grades, but make B grades.

The Side Effects Of Success

There are more things in store for successful people than just money. In fact what that money can bring isn't considered very thoroughly by people who don't have it. They settle in liking "the simpler" things. In being motivated it is best to keep an eye on the potential reward you will receive by trying. For some just one change in their lives would have meant a different and better life altogether. When I was a kid I had a good design for a new video game. The place I submitted it to showed a lot of interest in it. They said I would have to sign a paper before they could start putting it together. It was a form with legalities and on it you provided a brief explanation of the game you had in mind. I changed the idea entirely though. I called the idea "Dragon Slayer," instead of the previous idea of "Skull Brothers." My first idea, the one they actually liked, was about a skeleton with two heads, one with the power of ice and the other of fire. If they did relieve my original idea I could have been a game maker at the age of ten!

     It must be a fun life for those that make games. For those that have a say in it. The kinds of people that are always coming up with ideas that they know will be used. For everyone else wanting in, they could have the best of ideas but have the burden of knowing that their own thoughts are sort of useless. For the person who has made their way into the profession their thoughts are like treasure: worth something, even something valuable. That goes with so many other things. Those are the sorts of people with valuable thoughts. The ones with the power to create what they want to. Such as a singer in a successful band. The difference between the successful and the unsuccessful is that one knows they will be heard by many, and the other does not. The other just strums on the guitar hoping someday someone will actually hear. Do you see what I mean? It makes a big difference sitting down to write a script for a movie when you are a big person to begin with. The successful know that the people are waiting on their next big thing. The unsuccessful are riddled with doubts and uncertainty.

Being a success might include moving to a new and better city. It may be a big part of an overall plan. The successful have the benefit of living in the bigger and better cities, even by the bay.

They have more to give to their children and grandchildren. My grandparents on my fathers side always put together something wonderful for us, while they were still around. They had a nice large home to use for that purpose. There were rooms for us kids. There was an outside but roofed area for our large gathering to eat. The place was just pleasant overall. We were not celebrating Christmas and Thanksgiving in some run down overcrowded place. We got some good gifts on that day but we weren't spoiled. It was only during specific times of the year that we got things. One of them was at the start of school where we would get clothes in the mall or some place. Poor kids get into more trouble and sometimes have parents who have to get money in dubious ways. They go to school in the cheapest clothing. They don't have the things that make them popular such as a video game system and games. It's sad but true. If a kid is to grow up right then they need things like vacations, celebrations, and happy times to make it all worth something.

Wealthier people have greater legal protection. They have lawyers that are wisest and most determined in their profession. They are given things worth fighting for. That instead of some poorly paid legal defendant that really has better things to do than to work hard for him or her. So they have lawyers that can argue up a storm and intricately knows the ins and outs of the code of law. If they do go to prison they have an abundance of commissaries. If they are under house arrest, well, that is hardly a punishment.

They live long lives just as healthy as can be, for most part. They can afford the best treatment and the best doctors. They have access to "cutting edge technology." Their surgeons are masters with the blade. They can take house calls all they want. They are allotted the heavier expenses, not ignored a moment in the treatment they receive. They have healthier diets to begin with. Sure some of them get fat, and I guess that can be a problem towards health. But they have a broader and pickier diet. They get the best nutrition you can get out of food. They rest in better beds. They can have whatever expensive medication they need. They have visits to things like the spa and are sometimes in peaceful mountain settings without any kind of stress in their lives.

There are things that aren't even a concern to them. Losing power? Having to make things stretch, having to keep a car in order, having to drive at all, having to cook, not having hot water, cleaning their places, they have others to do that for them. They can be as loud as they want. They live in an isolated place on a nice hill. Certain moments never come for them. Like wearing out a pair of shoes or other clothing. Such as having to wake up early for a menial job. Such as waiting for the bus. Such as budgeting for food. Such as barely affording the bills.

When a successful person sings they sing before a sea of adoring fans. When a successful person writes a book they can depend on seeing reviews and personal opinions of it. They might even get to enjoy watching a movie that they basically wrote the script for. In a sense can be a script writer and a novel maker at the same time. When a successful person goes on vacation it is to Rome, to the Colosseum. When an unsuccessful person goes on vacation it is to a cheap hotel with a pool full of kids. When a rich person goes shopping they have the pick of the litter. They can buy the finest, the rarest, the intricately hand crafted, and the expertly tailored. When the successful athlete scores a point, the whole world is watching. And just from existing they are placed on things like trading cards.

Given the difference between the two we would all prefer to be successful. That would be mostly so. There are people in the world who curse their riches and walk out on it. There are people who choose monk lifestyles. If you are such a person I have nothing against you. You=less competition. But those who seek such greatness as I speak of have their own rocky road ahead of them, too.

Damn It When Things Go Wrong

I have made it a point to not pray for things. When I do pray for a better outcome or some such thing and I do not get it, I can get angry about it. "But you are all powerful God," and everything else like that comes into my thoughts. I also avoid self pity thinking. That can be such a miserable thing to have. "This shouldn't have happened to me," "I don't deserve that," "how wrong it was that ( ) happened." I also avoid paranoid thinking like "it was stolen," "they sabotaged me," or "they are out to do me wrong." I do try to hold hope. That it may not have gone as expected but there is a reason for that, is a better way to go if things aren't going to drive you crazy.

Fearful speculation is a thing to avoid. Never believe that there is only ever one solution to something. You'd have built up more worry than you would have had if it actually did happen. Something you long feared might occur and yet you find yourself dealing with it just fine. You even fixed the problem before you knew it, in a way you didn't know you could (because in worrying, you never considered it.)

It is like that day you were waiting for the mail all day. Then you suddenly realize it was a holiday. One of those holidays most people never even talk about. A lot of times in my life it isn't about getting something I want. It is about the relief of getting it when I do. It is more about to stop worrying then it is about what good it will bring. Sometimes during Christmas I think that my parents are going to forget me altogether or choose to not give me something that year. It is just a momentary and passing thought. They've always given me something. I always give them, my siblings, my nephews, and nieces, things. But for this nasty moment I think 'they aren't giving me anything this year.' Then the day doesn't even pass before it happens.. Like on Christmas eve instead, earlier than I even expected.

I'll tell you what made me mad one day. Having thin crust pizza delivered when I asked for pan pizza. Then this other time when I ordered pizza with some nice butter garlic sauce and what did my friend do? He opened it right up and poured it all over his pizza, leaving me none. Am still kind of angry about that sometimes. I used to get angry at the radio for playing dumb songs for hours at a time. Just when the song stops another and even worse one comes on. One time I went to the pawn shop on a Sunday. I was really needing some extra money. It was a long walk in a city without a bus. It was even a windy day. When I got there I asked myself why the hell they weren't open. Then I realized it was Sunday.

There have been times when my social security benefits didn't come in for some mystery or another. In fact during a time when I was homeless. That is a story I told before. I had shopped at a store with a data breach. At the same time I went to California my card was canceled and reissued to my last address in New Mexico. So I was shopping.. For clothing. As a Schizophrenic person I was obsessed with clothing. My card wasn't working. I thought 'must be the store.' So I tried elsewhere with the same thing happening. Then I went to an ATM. The ATM said something about a faulty card. That was at a time when I needed money the most. A time that, by the end, would lead me to eating from the garbage. Now my worst problem is that my allowance hasn't come in. I don't take it as seriously bad. I am honestly thinking about other things, like finishing up this book soon. At least I have some EBT money so I can eat. And at least I have a great deal of things besides. The only thing that bothers me at all is that I need to mail out the gifts I got for my mother's birthday. If I weighed one thing against another here then I am doing quite well.

I have chosen to become resilient for every good reason. I do not like being angry. It is a painful feeling. I do not like to suffer in self pity. I do not like feeling desperate. I don't like feeling hopeless. I do not like bad feelings. So I simply do not have them. I learned to not worry. I learned to not stress myself out with concerns. I just would rather live day by day taking from it the best that I can.

There Is Always Something To Hope For

It may have been a bad few days for you but just imagine how you will feel when everything does go right. You could have the hardest day ever but at least you have the bed to get into with a nice night's rest, and who knows if the next day is going to be better or not, but maybe it will be. There are always those things that can only happen in the future. They might happen only periodically but you can count on them. There are people with problems worse than yours. In fact there are people who would give their very life to live as you do. Some of us have good machinery working out good lives for us, yet we detest how slow it is. By comparison some have machinery that isn't working at all. Maybe it never even did. Maybe it broke some time ago. Maybe they were never even given a chance.

Taken as a whole, there is a great deal to look forward to. There will be days when you get things in an unexpected way. There might be a time you suddenly find a great new hobby. You might step through the doors of a brand new home someday, or at least a good apartment. Might even experience that a few times in life. You will have more birthdays. Christmas will be here before you know it. An awesome new movie comes out. Maybe something based on that book or old series you once enjoyed. You will have extra money sometimes, more than usual. "When one door closes, another opens." You might get a message from a long lost friend. There will be the first day of what will become a lifetime relationship. At the time you didn't even know where that would lead. You will be gifted things, you will be at restaurants some days eating some great food, you will have a trip to the ocean or some other great place.

Just don't let your problems be unsurmountable. At the same time do not entirely give in. Continue looking for solutions and fixes, but don't let a bad day come like doom upon you. Being strong and becoming strong is an important lesson in life. It can mean the difference from a greatly functioning person to someone torn apart and beaten by life.

Playing With A Full Toy Box

The older we get the less we do. A kid could enjoy a toy box for hours and for days, hell, for months. We could learn a valuable lesson from them. As the older we get the more we restrict what we use and enjoy. Yet we sure do pile up things with our new found money. We get those things that at the time we thought we'd use but never do. We are so limited in our talents for that reason, when there is so much to learn. We might not be into pretend play anymore, and call the toybox a tool box, but the same applies. At least some adults spend a lot of time on the food they consume. And many do have a solid and good woodworking hobby. For most of us most of our time is spent on a limited amount of things. Yet there are many treasures before us.

There was a time when I wanted to write so badly. I didn't even have a smartphone at the time. Back then those were just starting off. I had at best a laptop, but without internet. I couldn't post my books unless I went to the library, and they only gave you an hour. I actually went to a place where they let you use laptops for a limited amount of time. I took all the free wifi that I could get. Those were my restrictions. At a time when I had none of those I would write on notebooks hoping somehow I could get those into books. Since then that has been done by me. In fact I like making a good scanned-in-notebook-book. I use things like stencils, color pens, markers, pencils, stickers, and a spirograph set in making them. It is lots of fun. I used to wonder if these new smartphones had a word processor on them. Then I saw a commercial for such an app. I wrote for a long time that way. At least until I learned my books come out better when on a computer. The laptops I buy aren't gaming machines in any way. My requirements are rather simple. I just need to write with mine. With HDMI and modern TVs, I can even have a 43 inch monitor. So all problems were solved there. Along the way I found a wide variety of things to incorporate into my hobby, with more all the time.

I have a hobby I call "making prayer sheets," something I mentioned earlier in this book. It puts to use designer paper, neon color paper, origami paper, laminated paper, binders and paper, zip locks bags, color pens, envelopes, crystals, green marbles, foreign coins, sharpies, foreign bills, drinking bottles, staplers, stickers, glitter, stencils, ribbons, printers, and more. I never had a hobby that could incorporate so many different things. As for a tithe for my prayer sheets I might even do something like placing a small troll doll into the (gallon size) bottle.

I own a lot of stuff I may never use, however. For a time I thought my newfound interest in electronics would last. So I got all sorts of mini solar panels, a soldering iron, bread boards, switches, wire, LED lights, EL panels, and other such things. They have been collecting dust. I have a small sewing machine. Tailoring is one of those things I always wanted to get into but never did. When I was nineteen years old I was fully engaged in what I was doing. I would work out electronic knowledge on paper even without having any educational background on it. My father got a Windows 95 computer that I could use and I would type out this and that on it. I didn't have much. I liked to smoke and I liked Mountain Dew a great deal. I would walk to the nearest library and educate myself on various things. My small TV had a station on it where you could call up and pay for music videos to play. Although I never called in myself there were many that did and I would get to see those videos. I taped them on VCR. One time I decided to just make a big black candle. I took a fish bowl and melted all sorts of other candles into it, giving it a shoelace for a wic. At that time I would try to make ropes and musical instruments out of stretched cassette tape. My point is that I was so much more free in what I used to do. I was more interested in things. I wasn't at all limited in what I would do.

When I was a kid I would take index cards and make games out of it, with the best drawings I could make. I used to try to make video game magazines based on video game magazines. I used my talent for drawing the Ninja Turtles trying to make a comic book. In our earlier years we are totally interested in what talents we have. In older age it is just things we happen to know and don't really care about improving. We were so proud to share our drawings and do them better and better. Now it is more of a task. A thing like "let's do the best we can," without much pride alongside.

Maybe we can see the days again when every little thing in our room is neat to have and use. Or maybe it is just impossible to regain the interest in them that we once had. The older we get a thing is no longer looked upon with great interest and fascination, and that's just too bad.

The Art (And Joy) Of Buying

I used to be cursed with writing budgets. I would go through a hundred papers to "get it right." It was never right. If even my handwriting was off or a paper contained a mistake I would write it all over again. If I was ever OCD it was in that way. I would count the clock too for the moment my money came in. It would be midnight, and at one time I had a friend that would take me to Walmart.. At midnight. Then I had the problem of pawning what I did because I could not wait on having "new" money. I don't have those money problems anymore. I don't even cash my check until the next day. I don't hang on to the mail getting here. I can save some money. I don't have to know precisely what I will buy. I never sell my things.

There are different ways and styles of buying. You can buy according to a plan, you can buy impulsively, you can buy for others, you can invest, you can buy to collect, you can buy what you *need,* or you can buy what you *want.* There are a lot of purposes behind what you may buy. You may need some cleaning materials, some hygienic items, a thing to work with based on work or creativity, you may want something that raises in value or something to add to the collection, you might need more entertainment, or you may just want a good meal.

Let's say that a couple of miles away there there is a sale. You save, oh, 10% on something. You would rather not go so far out, however. The real question isn't if the trip is worth it so much as if the saved money is worth it. Is saving $5 worth the trip it takes? Some people couldn't be paid to go out a few miles, let alone to save it. Some in fact would pay the $5 if it meant they could shop closer. It is a quick way to waste money, sometimes. By going to a convenience store for food rather than taking the more difficult trip to the really good priced market.

Buying impulsively has its charms. It means to just decide what you will buy when you get there. It means to just buy what your heart wants. It is buying without any real reason. I know that every time I go into the store I am going to see things I didn't consider or knew that they had. Things that I wouldn't even think of getting until I saw them there. I try to put into any budget "anything" money. Like $30 towards "anything."

There are certain things we must always buy or else be miserable without. Such as a particular drink we like, food, things that let the day go smoother and easier, things that simplify other things, things we really enjoy, and things that keep it together. Then there are those instances when we must buy something. Suddenly the belt breaks, we are running out of dish soap or something else, and the daily necessities in life that we must have. We might have something for a week before we need more. We might have something for years before we do. Things like refrigerators are known to be long lasting. Not all things have that quality to them however.

Planning for the future is worth every effort. That means insurance. It means stocking up on long lasting food or other items, and it means investing. It could be to buy things that are only going to rise in value. It could be gold or silver bullion, rare things that there will always be buyers for, or just saving some money. I always spend a part of my food expenses on things that last a very long time. They are things I would not normally eat. If I was hungry enough, however, and out of food, then I would. You never know when a bad day might come so it is best to be prepared. If it is important and something you must have, always buy extra of it. The day might come when you thank the heavens you did.

Buying for entertainment is worth it. Especially with how much cheaper and better things are getting at the same time. Some still like those forms of entertainment that are going away. There are still things out there on the market for such people, however, and sometimes old forms return. Some are blessed to have a home where they can blast music on a great sound system. Some are in hotels with thin walls and maybe a bluetooth headphone set works better for them. Some are fine with old laptops and tablets they bought at a used electronic store. Some put their computers together themself. What is work for one person might be entertainment for another. Entertainment can be a hobby. It isn't at all limited to movies and music. For some it is a book. For others it is a craft that they know. Some get a lot of mileage out of a deck of playing cards while others intricately build a theater in their home.

Going to a store you haven't gone to yet can expose you to more things. Some stores are always changing their inventory. They are highly random at it sometimes. They are sorts of places where you will not know what they have until you get there. Flea Markets are the same way. Who wouldn't like going to a flea market? At one time these people had what they personally liked the most, and only for the reason that they no longer do they are selling it to you. Pawn shops have the same quality behind them: always changing what they have. As for certain online stores, well, the sky's the limit as to what you might discover. There are more stores out there than what people use. They are happy for your business and do their best with quality and prices. At least some of them do. I really like the online Goodwill store for one but I admit I use the popular ones a bit too much and should try new venues. New for newness sake can be its own reward even when it makes you go against a favorite and dependable brand. Sometimes it is just good to have something you haven't had before.

Some buy to resell. They collect things at a second hand store, perhaps a garage sale, maybe a thrift store, and sell it at a profit. Some have built things like complete video game collections by selling a portion of what they got at a profit, and save a few of it, then using that profit to buy more. Some of these are known as "pickers" and they have knowledge of getting things cheaper and reselling them. They might buy an abandoned storage shed's contents, go to some obscure place or another, and such things. They might be the refurbishing type. They might restore old things before selling them. Or they may add value to a thing like by doing a video game system mod.

Some are purely pleasure seekers with their money. I think that out of all the types of buyers I am the least like that. Some people like to live on fast food, like to spend a lot on scratchers and the lotto, see a theatrical movie if they can fit it in, spend lots on sweet drinks, with little more money spent on anything else. It is usually a once a month thing for them where they unload entirely and have to wait until the next month to do it again. Then there are those that add drugs and alcohol to all of it. They may have criminalized tastes.

Some are collectors. They want all of something. It may have started out by buying a little of any given thing and quickly became a large amount of it. Some are collectors without knowing it. If you have as many pens as I do, then you are a collector of pens. My collections of things go all over the place, not being anything specific. I would love to have a video game collection someday. I just can't get myself to start one. There is always the question among collectors and non collectors: why collect? If you aren't going to use it. If it is just there to be there, then why get all of it. I would just answer that by saying "why ask why?" People just want it to surround them and they love to buy it, whatever it is, and they don't need any other reason.

"You get what you pay for," and "buy it nice or buy it twice." Sometimes by simply paying a few dollars more you can get a much better thing. The question is, how much more are you willing to pay for something that is obviously better? I had to answer that question when I was buying a blanket. I had intended to pay a set amount. The amount would have gotten me this polyester blanket. Then I saw this one I really liked. It was King size and made of 100 percent cotton. That was fifteen dollars above my budget. So I looked for one better than the first one. I found one that was mid priced in it all. I kept going back to the much better one though and figured that this was a thing I would have a long time and use every night, so I will pay $15 extra for it. I took the large pure cotton blanket home and was happy that I did. Sometimes I go back and get a better product later. At the moment the cheaper thing might do but when I can afford a better one of the same thing I buy it. Then sometimes I do just to evolve the things I have. I look over things and make them better all the time in that way.

Then there is the question of what you are paying for. Do you need an extra feature? Sometimes you are just paying for packaging. Sometimes you are being downright tricked. Like with aspirin. Aspirin is aspirin. Generic sodium naproxen is the same as the name brand. There is no miracle thing. There is a lot of snake oil and people ready to rob you blind with their junk. When a product says it has this and that feature that I don't need, I avoid it. I am looking for quality *elsewhere*. Sometimes those are just gimmicks to begin with. They will say "comes from the finest mountain," "carefully hand picked," "made with precision, from the greatest metal," and things like that to pull you in. As for commercials I make it a practice to ignore them. I don't even read what they are selling or hear them out. They have more tricks up their sleeve then you could know. They would have you "hilariously" buy their product with a funny commercial. They would pretend to be on your side, your gender or race for example, making it seem as though that fake support should be paid for. They would make buying a car seem like the start of a great new adventure through mountainscapes. Just don't be fooled by any of it. Fortunately "made for TV" products can no longer trick people into buying junk, as there are many reviews a person can watch online, reviews made by real people.

Sometimes buying a thing means treating yourself. I normally don't like to spend money on fast food. The fact that after it is eaten it is gone keeps me from that. But I know to treat myself sometimes to some really good food. To get a loaded pizza or a Rueban sandwich can be very uplifting for me. Instead of this rolled stuff the real deal. To buy coffee beans and grind them for my coffee, that makes a good cup of coffee that will go on for about a week. My biggest example would be buying these two $500 dollar rings. One is 14k gold and larger than the other, with a snakeskin design. The other is 18k gold with a well faceted stone. It is just good knowing there is $1,000 in gold around my fingers. What I sacrificed to make that happen might have been just a couple of things that eventually broke down, anyway. If I take care of these rings they will last a lifetime.

Gift giving is the next topic. A wise person once told me that being serious about giving gifts helps you learn about your loved ones: what they like, what they are about. Mine is a box of truly surprising things that I am sure are loved. My gift giving isn't at all a generic thing. You could lose all that you have but never lose what you gave to another. At my age it is better to give than to receive. When I was a kid that was different. I am no longer at an age where I cherish things, where I fully enjoy them, or where they fascinate me. I know that children love whatever you give them, from the least to the most. I also like the concept that what you buy and give will someday come into the hands of another, and another, and another.. For example an action figure or a video game: It will have a long life ahead of it. It may end up in someone's collection for ten or twenty years. It may be a thing a particular person has sought out. It may come into great value some day, depending on how long it lasts.

I like to place cards and stickers into the gift cards I send out. Such as a favorite character for one of them in trading card form, could be NFL, could be show based or whatever else. The same with stickers. And I bought Christian bookmarks, cards, and stickers for them as well. If they were here in California with me then I would place lotto scratchers in the card. I mean for the adults of course. Sometimes I just grab a trading card that someone in my family would like and mail it to them. It doesn't add any to the postage, either.

Gift giving can be a competitive thing. One where you are either at top, the middle, or the bottom. I say that competition is fine and to try to be the best giver. Things like charity are good uses of money, too.

So build your little world. Have the things within it that will help. Have it contain things you will enjoy. Avoid pawning anything unless you have to. Buy the things you both want and need. Secure your future. Be ready for any problem. Enjoy your time shopping. Try to have two spares at any given time (so always have three of a thing). That is the magic number. Only make things better by evolving them and don't be afraid to step out of your comfort zone. Be willing to sacrifice just a little if it makes your loved ones happy. In all of these things your money will serve you well.

The Person With The Right Plan

Even the greatest giant fell to the person with a different plan.. A different approach, a different means. After that it would take hell to get them back on their feet. It is often the person that makes things cheaper, if not free. Things that are adequate enough without costing so much. The thing that meets the needs of others at a better price can turn many over to your side. Some had to find another way in. They had to rectify certain things. They just had greater talent perhaps in their delivery of it. They knew what was better and served it up. Nintendo for example, in the days of "the video game crash," had to find another way in. At that time video game things were considered a great failure. That is because games were being made left and right, each with way too low quality to them. It ruined the whole market in fact. Nintendo knew they couldn't even market their product as a video game system. They called it an entertainment system. They made it look like a VCR. They bundled it with "Rob The Robot" to make it look more like a toy. They guaranteed they would buy back any system that wasn't sold. And not until they did all that did they find their way back in. In fact they became legendary after that. More people knew who Mario was then they did Mickey Mouse. Nintendo was everywhere. They put up quality control limiting how many games a company could make per year. That ensured that game makers would spend more time on their releases.

So many other companies wanted to outdo them after that. They had things that seemed perfect on paper. They made products that usually just cost too much. They had ugly controllers. They had the littlest problems that kept them from getting into the market. They made systems that quickly flopped. The Nintendo Gameboy was inferior to other handhelds coming out, at least based on hardware. But the little thing that made them succeed was that their Gameboy's batteries lasted much longer. That and they just had better games.

There was a highly successful man in New Mexico that made gas stations known as *Allsups.* He is in fact the richest man in New Mexico for a New Mexico thing. He had a few things going for him. He had good prices on fountain drinks, he picked really good locations (with the motto "there's one near you!"), and he came up with the idea of selling fried burritos. They came with some taco sauce packets which went well with it. Everyone familiar with New Mexico knows about them and those returning to the state cannot do without a trip to Allsups to get one. He did well in providing what others did not. After the burritos came other things like taco burgers, chicken poppers, and even fried egg rolls, which is good when someone wants something different.

The person with the right plan is with the times. You could be at the start of any given thing that was subtly and quietly forming. Things that most of the world are not even so aware of at the moment. Like in the early days of the personal computer. There were those building them and selling them just when the market was getting started. Then there are those that are either against the times, behind on them, or too late. Sometimes things are just too well established to go against. Such as some online places and the video game market. Modern video game consoles require an enormous amount of talent and money to produce and market. Who can ever hope to do the same in a garage. At one time that was possible. It is certainly not the case anymore.

The person with the right plan has better ways of doing things. They offer a service that others never have before. Such as Walmart and their enormous stores or Amazon with their spend $25 get free shipping idea. I personally use Amazon to have tracking on all my orders, tracking that shows where the driver is on delivery day. Ebay was a novelty in its time for allowing bids to be placed. Roku offers free TV that is just as good as cable, only costing the wi-fi it uses.

One thing replaces another. Things are streamlined. They are done in better and easier ways at the benefit of the consumer. Capitalism serves all. It is in capitalism that the cheapest prices matter and the giving to people what they want. Competition exists within capitalism. Everyone has the opportunity to succeed under capitalism, too, so I would say it is a good thing. Not a thing where rich fat people only serve themselves. Quite the contrary. They got there by the need for them. Things once thought would go on forever find their end, often unexpectedly. So fewer magazines are being made. Great companies collapse. They invest all the time and energy into bringing about a new format. Some do anyways, unlike Kodak which did not invest enough resources into making digital cameras. More often than not only one format would succeed like going from records to cassette, cassette to CD, CD to the digital formats mostly being made up of the SD memory card. In the meantime we have monstrosities like the laser disk. There might be things that are cute such as the mini disk. Better floppy disks failed against CD Rom. Cart based games found their way out due to CD Rom too. You've got to master the overall picture to know which one is going to succeed and which is going to fail. You can't even count on the past in many cases. CDs were cheaper. They were cooler looking. They held far more data than floppy disks or many other storage mediums. But at the moment when digital files were needed more and more, things to store more than music, things that would do well with a smartphone, and to universalize the storage between so many different things, memory cards should have been the first place to start. People want something that will pack a wallop, that is cheap, small, doesn't cost an arm and a leg, and they need people to go along with them.

Whatever happened to the days of tinkering? The days when the mad scientist had things in their room to experiment with? The days of the inventor? The experimenter? Ironically the things they gave us made us content to just use what is already there and enjoy what has been provided by them. There was a time though when we lived in a dull and ordinary world but great things were opening up to us. Such things that we never had before were in the reach of anyone who wanted to be a part in making them. So much that could be done has been done. It is no longer an easy matter to make a good new electronic component. But there was a time when a battery was something new. Those came early on in fact. People were all over PONG when it came about. They used wood for some such consoles and computers too. They used parts laying around. These simple parts. Making simple inventions in their garage and becoming major companies later. Companies that had to evolve.

They say that the only good thing about internet explorer is it lets you download Chrome. That cable TV is going out. When vaping came out it was a miracle. It was considered so less harmful than smoking plants and paper. Unfortunately we are not allowed to know if it is safe or not– those that would demonize it won't allow a word to get in that supports it. After all, they have a cause to keep. They labeled it a "tobacco product." As a person that would benefit from vaping health wise, I suffer from the fact that in two day's time they were banned here. Sometimes solutions are not desired, to make my point. You have to have *their* solutions. They want nothing of you– you'd take away their income and lifestyle. It is like the doctor who does not get paid if there's a cure.

Sometimes it is all just in what a neat thing is made. It is the same thing only in a cooler way. There is something special to yours that others do not have. Your's might do the same thing better or it could just be that it only looks different. It looks better. It doesn't look cheap. Is based on a license. Like a Mickey Mouse watch. Like a Felix the Cat clock. Instead of a binder, a trapper keeper.

Advertising can go far. After all, it is an enormous industry. It can make the difference between being known about or not being known about.

Anytime you can find a cheaper way of doing something the better. Video game companies are willing to lose a profit on their consoles if the games for them are bringing in enough money. Sometimes costs are cut by things like not including manuals and producing games in disk based form. More and more they are coming out in digital form. Things seem to gravitate best towards cheaper costs. It is a double edged sword. It makes it more affordable to the consumer while making it cheaper for the producer. If you make something you make it and it is made. It is always there after it is made. A book for example, a song, or a video game. If it is a good one then it will pay for itself over and over again. You could have something that is licensed out. You could have made something that brings in revenue with no further work needed. Such as with really good old video games and video game systems. What was once hundreds of dollars to produce is now peanuts to produce. The games too, they cost a lot to make and had high expenses when they were created. Now though, a "mini" system could be made with dozens or more games pre-installed. That would have cost thousands of dollars at one time, but now sold for around 60- 80 $'s. So I would say work hard on making a good product. It takes one to enter into such a realm as that.

In all things, have fun while you are at it. A lot of things that were only dreams in the past are now in our hands. We can do so much more. We can do things that at one time required equipment we simply could not have, if it existed at all. We can have help in making things for us too. We could give a design and have that produced for us. Or we could get a good 3D printer to make it. That is so for whatever you are into. So have fun and be free in being a creative person learning along the way.

The Future I Hope For

I hope that things just get brighter and brighter. I pray for that. Some good new science and technology could do a lot of good. It could take our major problems and undo them. It could make life easier and better. It could make us healthier and live a lot longer. It can do a number of great things.

I hope someday soon that Universal Basic Income is set up. That would mean that it becomes more practical, which means that our resources increase. Those can increase from things like robotics, androids, drones, and faster food production. There might even be those food replicators some day. When energy is cheaper and more abundant, such as with fusion energy, guaranteed income becomes a more feasible reality. Homes for all: homes that are cheaply made with large 3D printers, and food for all, and all else we need more and more available, would be a truly great time in human history.

I hope that heaven is like Earth only amplified with all of our problems removed. That is such a thing that aliens could bring about. It is a thing we can bring about on our own, to be fair. I guess the truth is always fair. I once told a friend that science someday could make us immortal. He denied it. I tried to put it in his grasp with examples of how far we have come compared to a hundred years ago (and what about in a hundred more?) He pointed a finger at me and said "no! Man will never trump God!" I guess that was what was on his mind in making my point.

I pray for a time when greed has no meaning. That people can just have all they want and make of life what they will. One in which earth is a great paradise, a paradise even reaching beyond earth to new places. I kind of like the cyber punk thing as well though. Something like Blade Runner, perhaps. I myself have fears of losing my home and being homeless again. So a part of my own needs are in it. I hope that science will go more in the direction of limiting human suffering. I hope for science to expand and grow exponentially. It seems that is so, in fact. That things multiply more than they do just add. So instead of 1 plus 2, 3 times 2.

As for me there is certain tech I would love to have someday. I would like a really nice pair of augmented reality glasses. The kind that shows a large TV before your eyes. If I had some then I would no longer be bored anywhere. I live in a place where cleaners come in sometimes and I am required to be gone all day while it is happening. I would watch the downstairs TV but people come in and do strange things like comment on what is playing. They don't want it on the same channel. Some don't even want it turned on. But with a TV before my eyes with just a pair of glasses? Even a bus trip feels more like home. I could talk forever on how I would go on trips as a kid and how much easier and better that must be with modern tech.

I would like a mini computer that I could depend on. My needs for computers aren't much. Something I could put into my pocket. Something that I buy at the store at a fair price. I would never have to worry again about some complicated machine going out. I would just go to the store to grab another, even grabbing a few of them.

I would like speakers that beamed the sound directly to me. I could play my music and TV stuff as loud as I wanted.

I would like to stand outside and have food delivered by a drone. I would just step outside, order it on my phone, and in no time at all the little flying robot comes to me and drops off my food. I would like to go into a store and just grab every little thing I wanted and leave, with it being paid for through AI and things like that. It knows who I am and charges my card. That would be so cool!

I would like to rent a driverless RV vehicle. One that is driven using AI. To go onto a vacation with. One that uses electricity and goes places to charge itself. One that takes care of all the details. I would just pay a fair enough amount, get inside, until I arrive at my destination.

I would like seeing drones build great houses for the unsheltered. Skyscrapers. Those being built night and day with machines that do not tire and that know how to replenish their resources.

I would like to see the day when it is declared that a cure for cancer is found. Where the worst viruses are cured. Where cells can be renewed and people may live much longer. Where all of a sudden a great new source of energy is found and there is no longer any need at all to preserve it. It can just be used anywhere for any reason at any time because it is limitless.

I would like a great crime deterrent. One where people can no longer simply get away from committing atrocious crimes. An eye ever on such people, with nowhere to hide.

I would like a 3D printer someday. Making things like my very own action figures. For me those would be idols, not toys. I would make my favorite devils new and old. It would be cool to have a printer that simply does not need ink or whatever limiting and costly thing. The closest thing to that right now is a thermal printer, I guess, limited to the black and white, but at least the paper for it is very cheap. I like to print things out. My favorite images, mostly.

The days of the holodeck would be awesome. At that point humankind could take a small area and make it be without boundaries. I guess everyone would be just fine with a small room with a thing like that.

And I just look forward to those things I can't even predict. New things. Things that nobody saw coming. The kind of thing that is here in a day and everywhere the next. I am sure that science and technology has a lot of surprises for us. I knew nothing of the James Webb Space Telescope up until about the point it was being launched. A billions of dollars thing they sent a million miles from Earth (no kidding.) That was a pleasant surprise. So let it come one and all, today we are animals, tomorrow we are gods.

The Person At The Top Of Their Game

In the world there are first place people (and first place companies) and there are second place people, third place, and so on. There are more bottom place people than any other kind. Those make up people who don't even try. Making the very best does not come easy, to say the least. Some must settle on second best. They will either be surprised they did so well or disappointed. They may have thought that for sure what they have to offer will go to the very top, and some will either come close or fall far short of it. Let's compare Pac Man to Frogger here and Mario to Sonic. Then let's compare those to the ET Atari 2600 game and Bonk for the Turbografx 16. At least Nintendo is always doing what it wants to do. They throw it on the wall and see what sticks. Without such innovation we might not have things like the D pad or the thumbstick. Even in trying to copy Nintendo they fall short. They took the Nintendo controller and did what? They added one more action button to it. Then the SNES controller came out and there was nothing like it. They even had the insight to form the action buttons into a square pattern. While so many people were trying to make the next Mario they didn't come anywhere close to what Super Mario Bros. 3 was. Where were the thinkers needed for that kind of evolution?

I would call the bottom feeders the kind that take what another does to make money. Those that would clone an old idea– they know that it will get them some money. Not a lot, but enough for it to be worth it and easy at the same time. The bottom feeders are rip off artists. They copy the new sound in music. They have nothing new to offer. They might be too afraid to go against the curb. They are only as different as they need to be when it comes to patents. They take a very old public domain book and publish it online instead of spending time writing something new. They sell things like ROMS and Emulators as well as music, movies, and software made by others. They resell things that they found cheaper. They do so in the easiest and cheapest way possible. Those are bottom feeders.

People with a name brand are known the world over. It is often true that the first of its kind stays the most popular and copy cats have nothing against them. I find the second place commercials so amusing. Here is a fast food place that came first and brought about things that others would take from it. Then there are the commercials for others who would outdo them. They will pull every trick they can. They might even have much better commercials. Hell, the people on the top might even rarely come out with any. But I know that try as they might they will never be the best. They can come up with whatever novelty in food that they want. But they cannot outdo the best.

Some have the top brands and can charge what they want, basically. They can have it cost much more than the others. That benefits them in fact. It keeps the value of what they have in mind. For me, one of those things is Tide. While my clothes are just as well cleaned with other detergent, I prefer that over the cheaper stuff. Pods are very convenient too, and are an example of a good innovation. Innovating detergent can't be that easy. Such companies have to retain their quality however or else will sour their name. Companies such as Sony, who are renowned for good products. They even had a good innovation of CRT's. They came up with The Walkman. Had a hand in inventing CDs. Evolved the DVD into the Bluray. They outdid other console makers from the start. At the moment the Playstation 2 is the highest grossing console ever made. It is just a privilege of greater companies to sell higher, to make better, and to bring new things to the market.

Some companies suffer from just being part of a trend. They come and go like today from tomorrow. They might have had only one good thing to offer. And they will always try to continue that with a newer thing. The newer thing might totally flop. Then they are just gone from the market. They will try to stretch it out in the meantime. They will present things differently. Will come up with new commercials. But they could not improve, innovate, or come up with something new well enough to last. In the meantime they will try to come up with every trick in the book.

Imagine the surprise of the person who thought s/he had just a little to offer but then becomes a major success through it. They had a simple idea: one for a new kind of electronics, a kid's story (like Harry Potter), and maybe even George Lucas didn't think that Star Wars would do as well as it did. But in a day's time they go from nothing to all they'd ever want. Some people have such a spark. They have something they know in their heart will do well. They might even be mocked all the while being told that they will never go anywhere and they are wasting their time. It takes its maker to understand their creation. When people say "I wish I had thought of that," then you will know you made something really good.

Modern Controversy, Virtues, Vices, Sins, And Morality

There was a time when religion dictated these. In some areas of the world it still does but I won't be talking about them here. As soon as we started to abandon and outright reject religious guides a hole was created that needed to be filled. Great blasphemes arose, great freedom came about, and in no time at all you could find the darkest things possible on TV. In the 1980s the Satanic content on TV was objected to. Some of it was against harmless cartoons like the Smurfs. Some of it was against metal or D&D stuff. Some of it was very outright Satanic such as *Slayer*. Such objections no longer hold any power. In the early 90s the Mortal Kombat video game came out. That stirred some controversy. Enough to have games labeled for age guidelines. Controversy became a selling point. In the process of that the worst things that could be done have been done. I imagine it can only go so far until the novelty wears out.

It is no longer a sin to be an LGBTQ person. Not by society. Not where it counts. Not by law. Whether or not Christianity approves makes no difference. LGBTQ people can now get married and live a normal life without Christians getting in the way.

Intolerance is now a sin. That includes intolerance against other races, sexism, and homophobia. A whole moral code is built around it. It has become well known and labeled piece by piece and is something that many fight against. It is modern blasphemy and heresy to defame people based on those things.

Sexuality is no longer a sin. It is regarded as a harmless act between two people.. If it is harmless. I'm fine with that but I do not like things to be sexualized, personally. Which is fine, I can avoid those things that have been. It is a natural part of many modern mediums that I can ignore.

Selfishness is the new virtue. We live in a "what about me" culture. We are taught to make our own agendas and to not be obstructed from them. We are taught to devalue the opinions of others. We are taught to put ourselves first.

Smoking is a sin. Through lots of propaganda it is preached against. They found that the most effective propaganda against it is by making it look disgusting. I myself have smoked in secluded areas where someone would come right up to *me* and say "put that disgusting thing out!"

Modern controversy is in the more racist, homophobic, and sexist things. Violence has been done time and time again and people have been desensitized to that and cussing, and other things that in the past were not allowed, but are now everywhere. Things like those are no longer controversial. There is no one stopping them from being included on TV or online. For sexual things, the same. *Modern* controversy must be tough: like a coffee store called "I love Satan's" which has disposable cups covered with Satanic imagery. The inside of which has clearly Satanic music booming in it. A lot of it is just when you ridicule a person just for being who they are. I like to think that Christian Satanism could be startling upon its presence.

Being successful, becoming rich and famous, is a modern virtue. "All rich people go to hell," is not a thing that modern people would ever say or think. To look at music videos, a lot of it is about being wealthy and bragging about it. It is the greatest goal in life: to get rich. Some people like to show off the snacks or good meals they have.. Making others envious that way. Striking envy has become more common than ever. People want the greatest phone to show off, the best shoes, the best jewels.

Exercising and living well are modern virtues. Protecting others and others protecting others.. Being careful as to not harm anyone, those are modern virtues. Hygiene and self care are two more important things among today's people. Diets are very much promoted.

If people don't "understand" then that can get them into a lot of trouble. That means sympathy and empathy. I guess that is one thing that hasn't changed. Love is still a virtue.

Having Fun With What You Buy

I once made a door curtain out of plastic straws and thread. It came out even better than beads that would do the same thing. Having a sense of crafts can add a lot of fun to what you buy and use. A lot of it can be done at a cheap price too. So whenever you are in a store pick up a few random things. You never know what will come to your mind in bringing it together.

Origami is a lot of fun. When I was in grade school there was no internet to learn different origami things. So as an adult I finally had the chance to learn a few things. I remember in school people would make these awesome things like little frogs and now I know how it is done.

Putting together a puzzle or a model are two other things. They can be Legos too. Maybe you might like working on electronics and have a simple idea in mind. Maybe getting a canvas and paint to paint with would make a good afternoon for you. Maybe you might want to try leather work and there is a leather store with equipment for you nearby. I actually tried that one at one time.

I can't stop by a capsule toy vending machine without putting in at least a few quarters. Those are hard to come by anymore: at least where I live. The same goes for a claw grabbing machine. I got a stuffed snake the last time I used one. I am not too bad at those things.

Going to a comic book store and getting random comics, just the ones that look good, or based on some education about them if you have it, can be a fun time. The same can be said of a bookstore.

I like a store that has randomness to it. Things like antique stores that have different things all over the place. As for antiques there is often more style and work put into it. The best choice in a today-store might be made up of plastic or mass machine produced.

My family would go to Pizza Hut every Thursday. We'd always get the Pan Supreme. Best Pizza on the face of the Earth! They have a sort of fried bread flavor crust to them that the other pizza places don't. They have large containers of parmesan cheese that you can pour out at will. The only thing they don't have is the butter garlic sauce that Papa John's has. Then again, maybe things have changed. I haven't gotten anything but Dominoes in the last few years because of my new living arrangement. I used to mind going to a restaurant all by myself. It even felt embarrassing being alone in one. I don't know why I used to think so. Doesn't bother me a bit anymore.

There was an exploratorium kind of place my family would go to. It was in Amarillo. San Francisco has a much larger one. It is called the exploratorium here. I don't remember what they called it in Amarillo. It is a science place– mostly of interesting science tricks, tricks in physics. Like a thing that generates a tornado. A thing that flashes your shadow upon a wall. A thing that makes a beach ball hover above a fan. A dome to roll a penny down very slowly and circularly. It was fun to wade through all that stuff. They also had a special theater. It had a half dome shaped screen above you. You watch the movie above you more than you do straight ahead. It was loaded with speakers too to give it a special surround sound. They fit science in it all by showing nature based videos. It was really engaging.

Some like to fish and will buy every piece of good equipment they can on it. They have their favorite baits from natural to synthetic. They have their favorite polls. They might go fishing on a boat or at a river or wherever else. Some like to golf. Some like tennis. Some like pool. Some like pools. I used to do a lot of skating. I could zip around the lap at high speeds without ever bumping into people. These days I am a more excuse me type of person. I am too old to enjoy something like that. I am too old for amusement parks. I am too old for a lot of things so enjoy it while it lasts.

Arcades used to be a pastime before they were replaced with powerful game consoles (and not to mention much larger TVs.) I spent a load on nearly beating an arcade game and that is a good memory I have with one of my siblings. It was the Terminator 2 arcade machine with two guns. I did beat the Aerosmith arcade machine which was a two gun game too. I beat it with an ex-girlfriend of mine. I never had so much fun though as I did with the NES and SNES. To no longer have to put quarters in and to play to your heart's content was a great deal of fun. I really enjoyed two player (actually four player) Mario Party games with my siblings. That and Guitar Hero were loads of fun with my family.

I bought a Mickey Mouse children's umbrella just to have it. I passed by a unicorn rainbow snow globe that I couldn't resist buying. Sometimes a pen seems like an extra special pen. Sometimes a tumbler has such a neat design on it you might want it. Then in looking for clothing you find things you totally want. Like with shirts that have a special old thing on it. My generation clung to nostalgia more than any past generation. It was probably due to the internet giving us access to every old thing. That goes for both entertainment and collecting.

Some people cannot wait for the weekend. So they prepare for it any way they can. They might get snacks. They might rent a movie. They might buy some beers. They might be up late that night partying with a few friends. Then the wretched Sunday night comes along and the new work week looms over them. Saturday morning for me as a kid was watching Saturday morning cartoons and playing the game I rented Friday. Sometimes I would go to the library. I would get way too many books. Even as a kid I had my own library card. Across from the library there was a comic book store. They sold old comics very cheaply. I would go there on my bike often, using a few dollars my dad gave me. Then one day I went there and it was closed. I was too young to realize it was permanently closed but figured that out after never finding them open again.

Halloween can be a fun time of dressing up whether you are an adult or a kid. Picking out your costume as a kid was a cool thing. I had a very traditionalist grandmother but even she didn't mind if I dressed grotesque, like Jason, with fake blood on a hockey mask. My most common costume has been The Devil. Having a horned mask with that red face and beard, and a plastic pitchfork besides. Who tops Satan as the greatest monster? These days I like to collect things that are only on sale at the time. There are a lot of things there that aren't around until it comes.

Try some board games or some card games. Find a gamer to game with. Learn D&D or Magic The Gathering. Play dominoes if you prefer. Play Hearts or Rummy or some kind of card game. Play poker with whatever to gamble with. There are more games of these than can be counted. There is always a different one to play. Normally the rules are easy enough to grasp and catch on quickly. One of my favorite games brought together a lot of it: it is called *Clubhouse Games.* There are also games you can play on your own, such as Sokoku. Thanks to the internet a person can have a game partner whenever they want.

If you really want to go to extremes: build a pool. Put together a home theater system complete with surround sound and a nice long couch. Buy an ice maker if it makes things easier and more dependable for you. Get an extra large TV. Get the newest game console and a gamer's chair. Get a powerful computer. Get ready to take part in the best game of today's time, finishing it like a completionist does. Get an expensive device that can lead to fun uses: like a good 3D printer. Improve your home in the best way that you can if that interests you.

Or if you want it cheaper: start a new series of books. Get a free to play game. Get a "classic" game. Buy an old magazine to flip through. Start a comics subscription. Gather the ingredients for a good dinner or family BBQ. Buy some red wine or just some cheap vodka. Go see a movie in the theater. Go to the bar or a restaurant. Have fast food delivered to you. Buy some exercising equipment: like dumbbells and stretch rope, you could even skip rope if you want. You could start a martial arts class, or yoga, or Tai Chi. You could as well attend a class on any given thing. Then there are mini vacations you could give yourself. If you are in a crowded house then renting a hotel for a few nights might be nice. You could even take the bus to a larger neighboring city to do it, and find things to do along the way.

Don't Let Me Get To You The Wrong Way

I have high standards. I might come across as having standards higher than I really do. But my standards may be useless to you in one way but too restricting in other ways. I have provided the answers I needed myself during my lifetime. They may or may not apply to you, and keep that in mind. I am not a do-as-I-say kind of person. I am much more a here-are-different-ways-of-doing-things kind of person. I am not a religious person here making dictates. I feel that knowledge should be free. I feel that closed mindedness can be a bad thing. I look into the light, dark, and gray. I present the light, dark, and gray.

Unlike so many religious leaders before me, I do not present myself as the only one who should be listened to. I do not claim to have the ultimate and end-all knowledge. I do not make myself appear that I am even gifted, really. So within what I do I do not have a monopoly over it. Good people lead to better people. That is evolution and progress. The student outdoes the teacher. That is the way that it is. I simply say "choose your leaders yourself, and do not let another force you into being their student." So look for answers all over the place. There will always be that person who made any given thing better than what the original person made of it, if that makes sense. Sometimes I am vague in what I say intentionally, leaving room for growth.

I've never been a cult person. I have never sought dubious things. I don't desire to control others. My books are all free and in the public domain. I would refuse any interview. I would refuse to have direct control over my followers. That is because I don't get anything out of those things, it is because I don't desire them.

I wouldn't even say I am a lonely person who needs friends. I am fine with being alone and I prefer it. I would probably not want to talk to anyone on a daily basis no matter who they are. If I talk to anyone at all it is through my books and that is more than enough for me.

I hope that I have brought you a level of growth that you would not have found otherwise. I hope I have brought to mind things that you may never have even considered otherwise. I hope to have brought you those tools you need to be and do better. I also hope I am not taken too seriously. Just remember, the most important things you learn in life are things you learn on your own. Things are not too complicated in life. The rule of life is to just "live your best life."

But I have many books for you going over anything you can imagine. Remember that they are all free and in the public domain. If a publisher were ever to contact me and ask me to be published through them, I would turn them down. I would tell them "just publish it." I would like the public domain stature of my books to be taken seriously. I am not going to turn around and say "well you should have paid me," or "you should have asked for my permission." I do not want there to be any exclusive rights to my books. I want them to be as free as can be. One thing I would detest is if someone tried to take rights over them and prevented them from being distributed.

If I want anything it is fame. If the question was posed to me: would you rather have wealth or fame, I would certainly choose fame. I want to make a positive change. I want to make a positive difference. I want to be well known. I want to have something of substance that is used. I want to see the results of such a thing. I want to improve the world. And I want to be remembered. So you are doing me a favor by freely sharing my books, posting them online, commenting on them, rating them, reviewing them, and so on.

You can look forward to new books too. I am a prolific author. Before long I should have 60 books out there. Technically I have already written 60. 50 means 50 good books. 60 means plus some bad. And I took away the bad and improved on the old, combining some of them together for a thicker read. So I call it "50." This one was finished on January the 12th, 2023 (43 A.C.)

And thanks for reading.

About The Author:

I was born November the Eighth, 1980 in Raleigh, North Carolina. As an infant my family took me to Portales, New Mexico. I would soon move to Clovis, New Mexico where I lived until I was 10. I then moved to Texico, New Mexico. The following years I would live in various cities and states. Because of going back and forth in general and trying to learn who and what I was, I drew the conclusion that I was gray. I adopted the label of Christian Satanist and wrote my first book: *The Christian Satanic Bible.* In my mid twenties up until just six years ago, I was wandering around all the time. I have lived in just about any living setting you can think of. My wisdom came from my madness. Once I recollected myself I could go back to it and sort it out. It gave me a source of knowledge that would allow me to write things quickly and easily. It was of things that were not before me and may not have ever been without me, such as my *List of the Principality,* a thing I came up with while in strict isolation: in a jail cell, a "rubber room" for a month's time, inflicted with Schizophrenia. I became homeless for a year wandering around San Francisco in depravity. I made it through and now am an able body and able minded person.

I have always been interested in writing more than anything else. As a teenager I would spend my small allowances on pens and paper. When I did have more money I would buy better pens and better paper. I went from paper to mechanical typewriter, to electronic typewriter, to desktop computer, laptop, smartphone, and back to laptop. I was always delving into the more occult and religious side of things.

I had a side interest come about, that of retro gaming. I do not play very many video games but am very interested in watching videos from others about it online. Now I spend my days in comfort. I have come into a nice living arrangement. I have every little thing I could need. My life cannot be better. I have lived here in San Francisco for nine years now. This Saturday my new team is playing my old team. From age 10 I liked the Seattle Seahawks. They are playing the 49ers. But my point is, I just like ordinary things the same as everyone else.

I am just a person that hopes and prays his life continues to go as well as it has in these more recent times.

About My Other Books

My books are found under these names: Lucifer White, Lucifer Jeremy White, Lucifer Damuel White, Lucifer Jeremy Damuel White, and Adam Jeremy Capps. You might even find some under Adam J. Capps and Lucifer J. White. Usually my video game idea books are under my birth name (Adam Jeremy Capps.) While the Christian Satanic things are under Lucifer Jeremy White. The more Satanic under Lucifer Damuel White. For most parts my books are under Lucifer Jeremy White. I am specific with these because typing in one variation can either bring a book up or not.

Christian Satanism? It is a gray sided religion. It can also be about being both, or about being a Devil Worshipper. I leave the definition up to the follower. It is a non-sided thing that considers both over just one. Some however just like my Satanic books. My "Lucifer's Satanic Bible" is popular, as far as sales go. Then I have my video game idea books. A lot of that is made up of all new ideas for any new video game. What it would contain, how it would do things, how something or another adds quality to it, most of all. My "Antichrist Game or Movie" is a book mostly about making a Satanic video game. I have books about five imaginary planets. There is The Bible of Mother Aeon which is its very own thing. Then there were some things I was playing around with such as "Godism" and "Crazyism." Crazyism is a crazy way of spelling it! Godism is mostly futurism elaborating on what the future may bring.

I have scanned in books too. Most of them are in my "Lucifer's Notebook" series. There are five of those right now. They are hand written. I included stickers, used stencils, color pens and markers, and a spirograph set. It is just a fun way of writing for me.

Once more: my books are all free (as ebooks) and in the public domain. So please share them! If you want to see me on YouTube it is under "Christian Satanist Lucifer White," an easy to find channel. It is mostly made up of playlists. I have been putting out videos of my books as they come along. So on that channel you can see what new books have been made and when they are available.

And once more, thanks for reading!

Lucifer Jeremy White

A List of My Other Books:

Christian Satanism and The Herald of Satanic Waters
Christian Satanism and Christian Satanic Doctrine
Becoming a Christian Satanist and Mastering Christian Satanism
The Christian Satanic Bible
Another Christian Satanic Bible
My Antichrist Game or Movie
The Satanic Book and Satanic Living
Satanic Poems 1-310
Branches of the Satanic Tree
Lessons of Demonic Magic
The Bible of Steel
The Bible of Mother Aeon
Christian Satanic Books 1-5
Godism (series) Crazyism (series)
Books of the Five Planets (series)
Lucifer's Books of Inventions and Ideas (series)
The Game Maker's Bible
The New Video Game Idea Book
The Christian Satanic Book: An Introduction To Christian Satanism
Lucifer's Notebook (series)
The Christian Satanist
Lucifer's Satanic Bible
Making a Great Video Game
Introduction to the Five Planets
Christianity, Satanism, and Christian Satanism
Alien Messages for a Christian Satanist
Book of the Satanist
New Ideas for Video Game Things
Lucifer's Light, Dark, and Gray Sided Book
And now: Lucifer's Great Book.

Hales- Nema, So Noted In Memory.

www.ingramcontent.com/pod-product-compliance
Lightning Source LLC
Chambersburg PA
CBHW052038280526
45791CB00010B/3000